# Return to the River

## A STORY OF THE CHINOOK RUN

by

Roderick Haig-Brown

*A Totem Book, Toronto*

First published in Canada 1946
by Collins Publishers
Second edition published 1974

Re-issued in 1982
by TOTEM BOOKS
A division of Collins Publishers
100 Lesmill Road, Don Mills, Ontario

**Canadian Cataloguing in Publication Data**

Haig-Brown, Roderick L., 1908-1976.
  Return to the River

First published: New York : Morrow, 1941.
ISBN 0-00-216836-7

1. Chinook salmon.    I. Title.

QL795.F7H33 1982        597'.55        C82-094206-5

Printed and bound in Canada by
T. H. Best Printing Company Limited

# RETURN TO THE RIVER

## Also by Roderick Haig-Brown

# FOREWORD

The lives and deaths of Spring and the other chinook salmon described in this book occurred more than thirty years ago, in the early stages of the orgy of dam-building that transformed the Columbia from a magnificent river to a series of freshwater impoundments. There never has been another such river on the face of the earth; there never will be again until all the dams have rotted out and washed away and some thousands of years of healing time have passed—perhaps not then.

The Columbia system was at the very heart of the chinook salmon's range and so favorable to the species that chinooks ran to it in every month of the year and in three major waves —spring, summer, and fall. There was nothing random or capricious about these runs; each was a sub-race precisely adapted to the conditions of its own part of the watershed. Each produced its own kind, with the homing instinct and the strength and stamina needed for return to the stream of origin, a natural adaptation to temperature and flow conditions and a precise timing of spawning, hatching, and downstream migration that assisted survival.

Many, very many, of these stocks have been wiped out and it is unlikely they can ever be replaced. Dams have blocked off more than 60 percent of the Columbia's spawning areas; pathetic remnants of the runs still struggle up past some of the dams and into the distant headwaters: two or three years ago I watched a few spawning chinooks far up the Salmon River in Idaho, a sad little shadow of the runs of old. No fish at all run above Grand Coulee, so the runs of eastern Washington, northern Montana, and British Columbia, the mighty fish of the summer "hog" runs, are no more.

The hardy persistence of some of the up-river races, true native stocks, would be encouraging were it not for the steady attrition that drains away their strength season after season, year in, year out. Migration delays of both upstream adults and downstream juveniles, at the dams and in the long slow reaches behind them, take their toll. Young fish are destroyed in the turbines and spillways and by increased numbers of predators in the impoundments. There are heavy losses, in some years very heavy losses, of both adults and juveniles in the nitrogen-saturated waters below the dams.

Perhaps ways can still be found to counteract these effects; man is not much good at helping the fish, but he is learning slowly. If so, the fish will do their part; they will persist, perhaps even increase. The remnant stocks might conceivably develop new tolerances for the changed conditions.

In the lower river below Bonneville there is still a fair abundance of fall chinooks, chiefly maintained by hatchery production. If no other evil is done these should continue and maintain a fishery. One bright spot is the "polluted river" that Spring passed through with such difficulty on her migrations. The Willamette is still not a clean river, but it has been improved to the point where oxygen levels rarely fall below the minimum requirements of salmon. Municipal wastes are now properly treated, and the pulp and paper mills are successfully treating most of their more damaging effluents. Power turbines are still a problem, though these too are now controlled and fish losses have been reduced. Small native runs of fall chinooks, coho salmon, and steelheads somehow persisted through the years of the river's abuse and are now being supplemented by plantings from hatcheries.

This is an achievement in recovery worthy of respect, one that can and must be emulated in thousands of other rivers all across the continent. It means that some descendant of Senator Evans may one day watch a descendant of Spring waiting for her time to spawn in the Canyon Pool. And that is altogether good.

RODERICK HAIG-BROWN
20 May 1974

# PART ONE

## DRAWN BY THE CURRENT

# Chapter One

I T WAS late September and there had been rain enough to raise the river three feet or more above summer level. It was still raining, not a heavy, savage rain but a caressing fall of wetness that had long ago set every leaf and twig dripping and now seemed to have the limitless, persistent endurance of a fine distance runner entering his second mile. It was rain that belonged to the time of year and the place, rain from clouds so low and untroubled by wind that the tops of the tall Douglas firs were dimly seen as though in an etching, black amongst white.

The river in its mild flood was impressive. It had run through the mile-long canyon, turbulently over its bed of boulders and against the steep rock sides, and now it came from the narrow mouth of the canyon, flurried white between the tall gray walls by a ledge of rock that ran out from the far bank. In the moment of sudden release it spread into a great wide pool, the white of its hurry lost in a current-creased surface. There were deep eddies on either side, under the lee of the rock walls, but the river slid on between them, forcing them apart, confining them above itself, until it had spread to a fan at the tail of the pool and claimed the whole wide bed for its flow. Then it was broken and white again in the long rapid that hurried down to the next pool.

The water was a little colored, not muddy but less clear than during the brilliance of its summer flow, and brought with it fallen leaves and twigs and dead fir needles. Most of the leaves twisted and swam and swirled a few inches below the surface—alder leaves, some black and rightly fallen, others still green, torn from the trees by winds that had brought the fall rains; maple leaves, sodden dark brown and fast breaking up; willow leaves, long and slender, some yellow, some black. Under the leaves, deeper in the water, were the salmon. The white patches of worn fins and scarred backs showed up first in restless movement, out of time with the rhythm of the stream's flow. Then looking more closely one no longer saw the surface of the water or the leaves or even the decaying whiteness, but only the salmon, long gray shapes over the round gray rocks and stones of the river bed.

The gray-brown of the river bed across the fantail of the pool was not uniform. From the lip of the pool where the water spilled over into the rapid below, right up into the deep water, there were patches of rocks newly disturbed by the powerful tails of the spawning female chinooks, paler gray than the rocks of the undisturbed river bed and with the summer's brown algal growth washed away from them. These

4

were the spawning redds, seed beds that were to produce their harvest of salmon in four, five, and six years'
time. Some of the redds were just started, small patches
of pale gravel with a female above each one vigorously working to excavate a better pocket for her eggs
among the stones and gravel. Others were larger, more
than half completed, and on them the females seemed
to work less fiercely while the attendant males fought
for position or waited like sticks on the bottom, set at
angles to the flow of the current, their heads turned
in towards the female.

Nearest the bank and only fifteen or twenty feet
up from the lip of the pool a large female rested alone
at the upstream end of her almost completed redd. It
was more than ten days since she had begun to work
on it and now she was nearly spent, with only a few
hundred of her ten thousand eggs left in her ovaries.
The redd was a large one, twelve or fifteen feet long
and more than five feet wide, following the line of
the current upstream. In it were ten or more pockets
of eggs, buried eighteen inches below the surface of
the disturbed gravel. She lay for perhaps ten minutes
with little movement, drifting down with the current
a few inches, edging up again almost without a per-
ceptible thrust of fins or body. Then she turned
sharply on her side, her body arched so that her tail
was touching the bottom. At the same moment her
whole body shivered powerfully and a strong thrust
of her tail sent her forward a little, disturbing a cloud

of sand and small stones which settled back over the rest of the redd as the current carried it down. She repeated the movement several times. Her belly showed whitely through the water and once or twice it was possible to see that her broad tail actually lifted small stones and threw them up into the current to be carried a foot or more downstream. Her last thrust drove her well above the depression she had dug. She righted herself and held perfectly straight with the stream, calm and unmoving as though the activity of a moment before had never been a part of her. Then she let herself drift gently back until her tail was well in the downstream end of the depression. She seemed to decide almost instantly that it was not deep enough, for she drove forward again and went back to her digging.

On the bank of the pool, leaning forward over a fir stump, an old man watched her. He was a lean, tall old man; everything about him—arms, legs, nose, jaw, eyebrows, even his coat—seemed long. Almost everything about him seemed also gray or brown; gray hair, brown face, gray clothes, brown hands, gray stockings, brown shoes; only his eyes were strongly blue in all the grayness and brownness. He was watching keenly, but not intently; one felt that this was an old thing, often seen but not to be missed. He moved fairly frequently, to rest a muscle or to gain a slightly better angle on the fish, but always smoothly and evenly in a way that would not disturb her. A pair of field glasses lay on the stump in front of him; for the time being

the strong blue eyes under the jutting, bushy brows
were good enough.

The depression the female was digging for herself
was now well over a foot deep and she righted herself
and rested for a moment as she had before, two or
three feet above the deepest part of it. Suddenly there
was a large male chinook near her. A smaller male
came across after him and a still smaller fish came from
the other side. The first male ranged himself alongside
the female, his head about level with her gill covers.
The second male moved closer, the big male turned
sharply and chased him off, then returned to the female. She had dropped down a little way so that her
vent was almost over the depression. The male lay
below her, rubbing his nose under and over her tail
for several seconds, then swam to her side again. The
smallest male moved closer and the second male chased
him away, following him right to the lip of the pool,
then came back and lay several feet below the female.
The body of the big male quivered slightly once or
twice. The female dropped back still farther, until her
vent was right over and well down in the deepest part
of the depression. The old man on the bank picked up
his field glasses. The big male lay alongside the female,
his body touching hers, his head about opposite her
pectoral fins. Suddenly both fish opened their mouths
wide and quivered violently. The female raised her
head, forcing her vent still farther down into the depression. But the old man, watching through the glasses,

7

saw for a moment the pink stream of eggs she shed. Then the white milt of the male clouded the water and hid them. The back eddy of the main stream flow held eggs and milt closely together in the spawning pocket. The eggs still had the stickiness of the ovaries and clustered together. A few fell away into cracks between the stones, and wisps of milt followed them. From upstream sand and stones began to drift down upon them as the female worked to cover the last egg-pocket of her great redd. She worked from directly above and from both sides of the egg-pocket, digging with her tail, and in about a minute the eggs were covered.

Under their covering they went about their business, absorbing water to increase their size and weight, losing much of their brilliant translucency, becoming harder, finally losing their early stickiness, settling farther down into the crevices between the stones. The small stones settled down on them, pressing them out of shape, forcing the main cluster to a flatness, separating more of the outside eggs from immediate contact with each other. But the eggs were strong and resilient to withstand such strains and many of them, down in crevices between the stones, rested freely in little cases of filtered water. Even when the pocket was finally covered by its full protective layer of fifteen or twenty inches of gravel, no single egg had been injured. There had been no escape from the carefully dug pocket, no escape within the pocket from the strongly searching sperms of the male. The female had completed her spawning in a single redd with a dozen pockets that averaged a thousand or so live healthy eggs apiece. She had lost a scattered hundred eggs in her digging exertions—eggs which drifted down to waiting trout or bullheads or huddled sterile under stones to die and float up to be swallowed by mergansers and goldeneyes and seagulls. Within herself the female held a further tiny loss: seven eggs unshed. As though concerned for them she continued her digging from time to time, working the gravel back over the last new pocket while she vaguely sought to make one more that would never be completed, never filled.

The old man on the bank was still watching her. Until this time he had never seen the thing completely, the fall of the eggs, the clouding, searching of the milt, the exact process of covering, the departure of the males to other matings and their own sure deaths in scarred exhaustion, the spent female still working above her completed redd. Many times he had seen the digging of the egg-pocket, the attention of the male, the outward signs of the spawning act, even the flow of milt tight held by the current in the pocket. But never until today the stream of pink, gemlike eggs, the cluster among the wisps of milt after the cloudiness had settled to its work, never—for he felt sure now that the female was wholly spent—the covering of the last pocket of a perfect redd, the supreme climax of a life lived through its full cycle to its logical end. The female was living, her body would live on in other bodies even after the movement of her gills and the flow of her blood ceased utterly. But her positive life was finished, the individual existence that had started with the fall of a translucent egg to the gravel five or six years earlier was over. "Death in a shell of life," the old man told himself, disliking the phrase even as it came from his mind. She was more than that still. Some trace of parental instinct held her there, something born of mechanical or chemical promptings, but something useful none the less, and perhaps having in it the germ of future development. If the abortive egg-pocket, never to be completed, never to be used, were not started, the eggs of the last complete pocket would be less well covered than those of the earlier pockets.

The old man straightened himself and drew his shoulders back to take the ache out of his bones. He was too old, too nearly spent himself, not to recognize the universal application of his thought; and it gave him comfort. Six years out of harness, he told himself, six years beyond usefulness. But I've seen that now, and I've seen other things in those years and enjoyed them all. One does not die inside a shell of life. So long as there is any life at all it is full life.

He started back along the trail towards his house, walking easily with long slow strides, his head down, his eyes glad, still seeing what he had seen.

# CHAPTER TWO

SENATOR EVANS had not meant to go straight back up to the Canyon Pool that afternoon. But in the house, during lunch and after, he was restless, his mind on what he had seen. He felt that he needed to know more of the big spawning female, whether she was still there on her redd, whether she would shed more eggs or whether it was really possible that some faint stirring of natural instinct held her on the redd after her work was done. He left the house quietly, almost furtively. They still came, those importunate men from his vigorous past, even now after six years, wanting him to do things—to speak here, decide there, persuade somewhere else. If one came before he could get away the afternoon would be gone and a chance to see something clearly and completely would be lost.

Walking along the trail among the alders and second-growth fir, he felt calm again, free to think slowly and clearly. He felt surprised, as he often had before, at his own strong interest in the chinooks. I am a fly fisherman, he told himself, and chinooks are no fly fisherman's fish. Steelhead are fly fishermen's fish, and they should be the more interesting—they have longer freshwater life, a chance of recovery after spawning and of returning to the rivers not once but two or three or even four times. Yet one loves the chinooks. They are the largest of the large, the strongest of the strong, the final end of what salmon can be. Perhaps that's what it is, just a normal American concern with the biggest thing of its kind in all the world. He smiled at the thought, accepting only a part of it. The chinooks were more than that; they were a proud symbol of Oregon, of the Pacific Northwest, of Alaska too and all the coast between. They were the abundance of an ocean and rivers and land scarcely known a hundred years before. A man bred in Oregon, here on a great spawning tributary, could not help but feel strongly about them. If he were a fisherman also he must love them.

The rain had stopped and the sun was out, not a strong sun but enough to make the mild day comfortably warm. The old man liked the light of it among the alders; it was on the leaves, not slipping through the frail green of them as it did in springtime—less lovely now perhaps, less delicate, less promising, but still a good thing, with its reminder of frost and ruffed grouse and the winter strength of the river. He walked slowly, looking about him, drawing the last sap of pleasure from the familiar things, the blue of sky between the living leaves, the brown of last year's leaves underfoot, the sound of the river, the dusty purple of the Oregon grape clusters against their stiff and glossy leaves. But his mind was still on the chinooks. One must love them for their fine strength and beauty, for the simple complete pattern of their lives, for all they are and all they represent. But more than anything else is the mystery of their movement, the carrying of the river out into the unknown parts of the sea, the long slow return, straining back to the source that bred them, bringing the fullness and might of the sea to the clear confining channel of the river.

He came to the pool again and saw at once that the big female was still on her redd. She was lying quietly, her tail over the shallow depression she had dug after covering the last egg-pocket. As he watched she moved upstream a foot or two, then turned on her side and stirred a little cloud of sand and stones with her tail. The old man noticed that her tail was frayed and torn; it no longer seemed the square and powerful thing it had been when he had left her a few hours before. A whiteness was showing through the gray skin and protecting slime. Watching closely it seemed to him that the movements of her body were less controlled, suddenly almost purposeless.

The light had changed and he no longer had a clear view of the river bottom from the burnt fir stump. He moved up to the rock face of the canyon wall and settled himself on a ledge at the foot of it. With the afternoon sun at his back he could see clearly to the round boulders on the floor of the pool; the big female, still quietly holding at the head of her redd, was in the center of the area of light. The old man loved this familiar watching post on the ledge; he had learned to seek it out in his most active years and to rest there, letting a young man's vivid thoughts crowd through his brain.

He had thought good things there and laid the foundations of good work. Now he thought more idly, watching with no stronger purpose than curiosity, holding the big female and what she was doing well to the front of his mind. But the habit of productive thought was still strong in him and he felt the need of more positive knowledge of what the big fish was doing. He could guess at the depth of the egg-pockets in the redd, at the number of eggs in each one, at the probable percentage of survival from the spawning. He had his own theory that the female was spawned out, that she was held on the redd in her dying hours by something nearly a maternal urge to protect. These things were satisfying, but they would have been more so if he could have told someone of them and found an opinion to check his own. He was afraid of his love of the fish, afraid of reading things that were not really there. And he thought again of Don Gunner.

Don might be down that way during the afternoon. He was always traveling up and down the river, visiting his fry traps, searching for food organisms, taking water samples, following one or another of a dozen experiments which had bearing on the chinook runs. It was at least partly in the hope of finding him that the old man had returned to the pool. So he watched and waited there, thinking of him. He thought of Don nearly always as he saw him in the laboratory—white-coated, with notebooks, microscopes, perhaps a rack of test tubes, certainly sample bottles full of small fish, slides with scales mounted on them ready for reading, and his own quick easy movement through it all. He saw him far more frequently beside the river or in an ordinary room or at a baseball game. But the vision of the white-coated scientist among the paraphernalia of his profession persisted. In the Senator's mind these white-coated young men were the symbol of America's salvation. He realized vaguely that his idea of them was oversimplified—intensely occupied, wholly devoted men in long white coats, research workers in all lines of progress, medical, biological, industrial, social, agricultural, geological—but he clung to it because it made him happy to feel that the secure, broad future of his country was in them.

"Incorrigible old sentimentalist," he told himself, and turned back to the fish again. She was moving uneasily, still in much the same position; her tail was working faster to hold her there and the motion of it seemed almost frail, driven only by the narrow rear part of her body instead of by the long full muscles of the whole of it. She drifted reluctantly backward a few feet, stirred herself and worked up again against the flow of the stream. The old man was leaning forward a little, watching her eagerly. He heard Gunner coming from the upstream side, skirting the canyon wall and working down to the ledge, but he did not look up until Gunner had settled beside him. Then his old face smiled, curving and redrawing the deep lines in the brown skin.

"I've been watching and praying for you, Don.

You're just in time to save me from my romantic self."

"A spawning problem?" Gunner asked. "The marital relationships of the chinook salmon?" There was no sharpness in the joking question. Rather it had a gentleness that argued a deep respect and affection for the old man.

"Not exactly a spawning problem. What happens afterwards?" Senator Evans pointed out the female and described what he had seen in the morning. "I'm morally certain that she finished spawning and covered her last egg-pocket several hours ago. But she's still there. What holds her and how long will she stay?"

"The females nearly always do stay on a completed redd as long as they can hold against the current."

"Could there be anything of maternal instinct?" The old man asked the question almost timidly. Biologists were such cold-blooded people and sometimes their rationalizations, even Don's, seemed to hurt just at first. Gunner sensed the old man's feeling.

"Maybe," he said. "We'd have to be very cautious and call it 'evidence of post-spawning parental care' or something of that sort. My best guess would be that it is a persistence of whatever stimulation it is that produces the egg-laying and redd-making activities. But the effect is the same in either case."

"How much longer do you suppose she will live?"

Gunner studied the fish critically. "She's still in good shape, but I'm pretty sure you're right when you say she's spawned out. That little patch of fungus on her

head will spread quickly now. She might hold somewhere near the redd for another week if the river doesn't
come up much."

"I never can believe they're so nearly dead when
you see them like that. How old do you suppose she
is, Don? Just give me an idea. I know I'm always trying
to make you guess at things you're not supposed to
guess at, but no one is going to pick you up on what you
tell me."

"It isn't exactly that, sir," Gunner said. "But I'm as
likely as not to be wrong on a guess like that. There
isn't much to go on except her size and the records of
scale readings from this stream. She's large—close to
forty pounds I should judge—and she's a spring-run fish.
The chances are that she's a stream-type six-year-old;
went down to sea at the end of her first year and has
been there ever since. But she could easily be a five-
year-old, or just possibly a four-year-old, if she went to
salt water at the beginning of her first year."

"How far out to sea do you suppose she went?"

"From the mouth of the Columbia? That's another
guess. Perhaps as much as six or eight hundred miles,
up off the coast of British Columbia. And then again
she might have spent her whole life within a hundred
miles of the river—practically within its influence all
the time."

The big female had moved a few inches towards the
center of the stream and was digging again. The current was carrying the stirred-up gravel down over part

of her redd. The old man noticed and remarked on it.

"You think it's a sort of provision of nature then?" Gunner asked. "To make sure the last egg-pocket is properly covered?"

"I like to think that," Evans said. He shifted his position a little on the rock ledge and looked at Gunner. Gunner's eyes were on the water and the old man studied him, delighting in the strong red face, the fine nose, sharply pointed, the high square forehead and the pleasant generous mouth. He knew the eyes, brown behind their big spectacles, and he read into the whole the things that he knew were there—energy and enthusiasm, the fanatical desire for truth, tangible knowledge, the ready imagination and the sweeping confidence in himself and in his work. The boy had rounded out, the old man told himself. He was powerful now and solidly set in the strength of his experience.

Gunner said slowly: "You know, there's often a lot in ideas like that. But they aren't easy to prove. Nothing about fish is easy to prove when you come right down to it. Look how many 'proven' things have been disproved in this century—the advantages of artificial propagation over natural spawning, for instance."

The old man nodded. "I noticed you were willing to accept that she"—he pointed to the female lying at the head of her redd—"might have traveled six or eight hundred miles up the coast and still found her way back here to spawn. I thought there had been some difference of opinion lately about the parent-stream theory and homing instinct."

Gunner laughed. "I'm glad you called me on it," he said. "I was forgetting. That one still has the boys with their tails in a knot."

"Talk about it," the old man said. "I want to try to get it straight." The afternoon was warm now, lazily warm for a fall day. There were other fish working over other redds at the tail of the pool. A lone merganser, flying fast from downstream, landed on the pool with a swish of water against feet and feathers. She had not seen the two men.

"You want to hear what I think?" Gunner asked. "Or just what's proved?"

"All of it, and give it some color."

"Let's start at the beginning then," Gunner said. "Here we are with a lot of research and a lot of conservation theories based on the idea that all salmon, or practically all salmon, return to spawn in the streams where their parents spawned. If you want to question that idea you make trouble for all the research and all the conservation work that is based on it. And you can make at least a show of questioning it, if you are really determined to."

"What about all the marking experiments? Surely you can't get around those?"

"No," Gunner said. "I don't think you can. That is, you can't get away from the mass proofs. We know, for instance, that the Columbia produces a lot of chinooks, and it gets a return of a lot of chinooks. We know that large numbers of them come to the river from five or six hundred miles up the coast; since the thing goes on year after year it isn't really reasonable to suppose that those up-coast fish came from anywhere but the Columbia in the first place. And there was the famous big sockeye year in the Fraser—it's not very reasonable to argue that such numbers of fish found sufficient food for growth without leaving the influence of the river in salt water. You can multiply instances like that."

"What more do they want then?"

"They want us to follow a fish by marking from fresh water to salt, then back to the same fresh water again."

"You get fish marked as fry in streams and recovered as adults in the same streams—they must have been to sea."

"Yes," Gunner said. "But not necessarily beyond the influence of their rivers in the sea."

"Well then, you get fish tagged in the sea off the British Columbia coast, then recovered in the Columbia. The influence of the Columbia surely can't be felt up there."

"No, but there's no mark to show that those fish were hatched in the Columbia in the first place."

The old man shook his head. "They want to have it both ways. And if that's all they've got against the parent-stream theory it doesn't seem to me more than a sort of negative doubt."

"It isn't quite all. There's some evidence of straying —of fish not returning to the streams where they were marked. A lot of it is from transplanted fish and I don't think that's worth much. But there is some straying under natural conditions."

"Still negative," said the old man. He spoke shortly, almost aggressively, glad to find that he need not discard a belief that added so much to his love of the fish. "It seems to depend on which side you think should bear the burden of proving its case."

Gunner smiled quickly. "That," he said, "puts the thing in a thimble."

"Then you feel you can trust the parent-stream theory—of course, pending further evidence."

"Yes, I do. As a matter of fact, it isn't so much the parent-stream theory that is attacked as the 'homing-instinct' theory—and I don't mind pulling that to pieces myself. 'Homing instinct' doesn't mean a thing anyway. If you do use the phrase you simply mean that something you can't explain or name brings a salmon back to its home stream. I believe there's an explanation and we're on the way to finding it."

The old man frowned and shifted his position. Gunner watched him pull out a cigar and light it slowly. "I think I follow that all right," the Senator said at last. "You think that almost all salmon get back to their native streams and that they may be guided back by factors outside themselves, such as currents and temperatures and perhaps chemical differences in the water, and that their response to these things will be conditioned by factors inside themselves—such as increasing maturity. You see"—the old man looked up and smiled—"I got something out of that last paper of yours."

"There will be some reactions to that," Gunner said. "Even though it was for popular consumption and stating what has to be proved rather than what has been. Naturally, I think what I wrote is not too far off the mark, but that doesn't mean a thing."

"What would mean anything?"

"As far as the Easterners are concerned, you mean? They want us to mark young fish in a river, recapture them in the sea well beyond the influence of that particular river system, mark them again and recapture them yet again in the river where they hatched."

"Could that be done?"

"Sure, but you would have to undertake a big expensive experiment to make sure of results. I don't know just what the odds would be against double recapture of a marked fish by the right people, but plenty anyway."

"Do you think the expense would be justified?"

Gunner thought for a long minute before replying. "I hardly think so. If I felt there was a legitimate doubt of the validity of the parent-stream theory, I'd say yes. But I can't help thinking there are better ways of spending the money as it is. Of course, the way the thing is put up to us is a challenge and makes me want to try it—they say: 'You fellows just produce this nice, conclusive, tangible proof and we'll believe you; mean-

while don't ask us to stop taking cracks at your stuff.'
In a way they've got something there. After all, we've
been trained to doubt what we can't prove up to the
hilt. Yet I can't help feeling that we've got pretty good
proof right now—call it a much better case than they
have—and that makes the whole thing seem something
of a side-track."

"Apart from those negative quibbles, just what are
their ideas?"

Gunner laughed. "I'll give you some really unscien-
tific dope on that," he said. "In the first place they are
big names—bigger, on the whole, than we average; that
means that people listen to them. And they are Easterners, not Pacific Coast men anyway—that helps too. And
really they are split. One claims that salmon never leave
the influence of their parent stream in the sea—or if
they do they probably never get back to it. As a matter
of fact, I think he's got his tongue in his cheek—he
has decided to show us up for trusting in something
that escapes a simple proof, stepping on our tails a bit
because he thinks that way he'll make us do something
good to answer him. Another of them is riding a chemical hobby horse—trying to explain salmon migration by
the responses of the fish to chemical conditions in the
water. Another wants to explain it all by currents. And
neither of these two seems to realize that explaining the
'homing instinct'—even if they could do it—wouldn't
necessarily wipe out the parent-stream theory. Then
there's one who throws up a lot of figures on trans-

planted fish that have strayed—turned up in stream
other than those they were planted in; the answer to
him is that transplanted fish haven't got a true parent
stream. There's even one inspired gentleman who finished off a paper with a beautifully documented refer-
ence to spiritualism as containing a possible solution.
He probably had a vision of the ghosts of old male
chinooks pointing the way through the seven seas, like
traffic cops."

The old man laughed. "It's good fun, though, even
without getting into the departed souls of the fish. A
grand problem and just one of those double recaptures
would be grand satisfaction." He was looking down at
the big female again now. She was still alternately digging and resting at the head of her redd, but all her
digging efforts had failed to produce another egg
pocket. He pointed to the redd behind her.

"How long before they hatch, Don?"

"There's a rule of thumb," Gunner said. " 'Fifty days
at fifty Fahrenheit.' Add five days for every degree
under that, subtract five for every degree over. This
stream averages something like forty-five degrees between now and spring; so call it seventy-five days—two
and a half months. About the same length of time for
the alevin stage up until the yolk-sac is completely ab-
sorbed, so you ought to be able to reckon a total of
five months before you have free-swimming fry. Some
time in March there will be a lot of little fish lying
among the stones on the bottom of this pool."

The old man saw the gravel come to life, little fish everywhere through the pool, working away from the bottom, darting out for food, finding favorite holts and resting places. "She's finished spawning?" he asked again.

Gunner considered the female. "Yes," he said. "I think we can commit ourselves on that. But we'd better take a look tomorrow." He glanced at his watch. "I've got to be getting back."

"Nonsense," the old man said. "Come along to the house for a drink and I'll run you up in the car. If I don't see you inside four walls once in a while I'll begin to think of you as the spirit of the river or something."

## CHAPTER THREE

THE big female held on her redd for three more days. In that time the fungus spot on her head, not much larger than the ball of a man's thumb when Gunner had noticed it, had spread down to blind one eye and along her back almost to her dorsal fin. Her tail had become a stump of white, naked rays, her white belly was unevenly darkened by runnels of blackish pigmentation. Through the three days there had been steady rain in the hills and the river rose as steadily, bringing down more leaves, more fir needles, growing a little dirtier and a little stronger all the time. As the force of the current built up, the female was washed back down the length of her redd half a dozen times, but each time she seemed to find in herself a sudden strength, born of panic or perhaps of the same urge that had driven her down from the north, through the long reaches of the Columbia and into its tributary to spawn, which let her struggle again and reach her favorite position.

By mid-afternoon of the third day she was very weak, and the river current was brown and strong, healthily brown and strong with a richness that seemed to belong only to young and vigorous things, in which she had no part at all. She struggled against it, even turned on her side once or twice in a pitiful caricature of the powerful digging thrusts she had used to make her redd. The current caught her and rolled her over. She struggled against it, righted herself, but she was unbalanced and her gill covers opened in wide gasps. The current caught her again, swung her broadside, carried her down the length of the redd and out over the lip of the pool. In the broken water of the rapid she was tumbled and tossed, no longer out of time with the rhythm of the leaves and debris in the river. She was thrown into an eddy behind a rock and found strength to thrust out from it with a drive of her frayed tail. The current rolled her over, swung her into another eddy close under the bank. She hung there, belly up, her gills moving a little, her under jaw breaking the surface of the water as the wavelets from the rush of the rapid lifted her.

The rain went on and the river rose steadily to full autumn freshet, tearing at the canyon walls, rolling the boulders along its bed, foaming in three great crested waves over the ledge at the mouth of the canyon. It swept in smooth strong flood over the tail of the pool, over the female's eggs, her vigorous living body deep down in the gravel. A man, taking one of the eggs between his forefinger and thumb, might have burst the shell and scattered the life from it with little effort. The mere touch of his hand, carelessly stirring the eggs under water, would have killed many of them. Yet under the uncontrolled weight of the flood, under a foot or more of settling stones and gravel, they were safer than they could have been anywhere else in the world, with a mathematically better chance of life than any ingenuity of man could have given them.

Here and there in the river there were redds that did suffer from the flood. It was a stronger flood and a dirtier flood than the fall freshets the river had known before the timber was cut away from the hills. It brought with it clay and earth in suspension and deposited them in choking silt wherever the current slackened. The redds built in too sheltered places were buried and the eggs in them died, sooner or later, suffocated because the oxygen-bearing water could not filter through the silt. Over some places the flood rushed too fiercely, scouring the gravel, rolling the heavy boulders, breaking up the redds, exposing and scattering the eggs so that the trout and bullheads found them or they died and at last floated up for the seagulls and ducks.

While the flood was still running hard Senator Evans stood with his wife on the banks of the river near his house. The force of the flood and the dirtiness of the water saddened him, and he pointed down to the brown surge of it at the foot of his lawn.

"That's what's happening to America," he said. "That's what we've done to her."

Edith Evans knew well enough what he meant—she had heard it before many times—but she did not care to let him reproach himself; it wasn't good for him and he could slide too easily into denying the value of the whole work of his life if he was allowed to dwell on it.

"It has made a great country," she said quietly.

"A great country and a great people," he agreed. "But faced with tremendous difficulties. Nothing the pioneers had to face can compare with what the Americans of today have to face."

"Don't be so gloomy about it, Tom," she said. "They'll face it and find a way out. Anyhow, you don't have to take it all on your poor thin old shoulders."

He laughed and touched her hand under his arm. "No," he said. "I guess I don't have to take all the blame for the rape of America. But it's people like me, and worse, that let it happen. Some of us were just plain dumb or didn't care, some of us thought we were doing the right thing, even a glorious duty. And some of us knew damn well that it wasn't all just right, but there was money in it and that was enough."

"Go along for your walk, Tom, and don't think too much about it." She drew her hand away from his arm and turned back towards the house.

Evans walked up the river to the pool at the foot of the canyon, as he did once or twice a week all through the year. He climbed on to the black stump on the bank near the tail of the pool and sat so that he could see the white water foaming against the rocks a hundred yards up the canyon. Every so often he turned from that to look down at the strong surge of brown water over the place where the big female had spawned. It seemed hard to believe that anything could be safe down under that force and weight, yet the old man knew it was a good place, as good as any in the river. He wished he could see down to the rocks and judge somehow what was happening; the spawning of the big female had touched him deeply—and he did not care to feel that now it was over for him, that he would never know anything more of it. He sat on the stump for a long while, a far longer while than usual, before he went home.

The big female had chosen her place well. There was silting in the big pool at the foot of the canyon—behind the rock ledge and in the eddies at the sides. And there was scouring in the rapid below. But the smooth strong flow of water over the fantail of the pool, almost even from surface to gravel, scoured very little and drew most of the silt on with it. Where the friction of the bottom slowed the current above the redd, where tiny eddies formed behind the small stones, there was some settling of fine clay and sand, but little more than enough to recement the disturbed gravel and form a light crust over the loose stones of the redd.

In the main body of the redd, between this crust and the undisturbed bed of the stream, there was a stratum of clean gravel through which the oxygen-bearing water filtered freely. The eggs, deep in their pockets, were safe in this, washed by the clean water, cushioned by it, fed by it. They had already passed through several stages and in each they had found full protection, not only through the female's choice and careful building of her redd but in their own mechanical adaptability. Dropping from the female they became briefly hardy, resistant to the dangers of concussion and suffocation, receptive of the searching sperms of the male. Held tightly in the egg-pocket by the current and by their weight, kept together by their own quickly passing stickiness, they were readily found and penetrated by the fertilizing sperms; then the outer membrane, the chorion, of each egg took on the tremendous degree of elastic strength which protected it through the filling and settling of the egg-pocket.

The egg from which Spring, the salmon of this story, was to hatch was one of the main central cluster in the upstream pocket of the big female's redd. It was an unremarkable egg, lost among a hundred others exactly like it. Inside the chorion was a narrow space completely circling the real egg; within this was a second membrane, very thin but holding within itself a number of oil bubbles and thickening where the sperm of the male had entered to a flat disc which was Spring. Within this again was the yolk, a pale-yellow transparent mass, and for the time being Spring's life was the process of transferring this yolk into her forming body.

A short while after the egg-pocket was completed their protective hardiness left the eggs for about ten days. During that time a single egg died in the upstream pocket of the redd. It was one of a tiny group of a dozen or so eggs on the extreme edge of the pocket and it was lying loosely in a small irregular case made by the piling together of a few stones of considerable size. In this case it moved constantly to the flow of water through the redd, bumping against the stones until the concussion killed the life inside it. Almost as it died the egg changed visibly. The yolk congealed as the salts drew out of it, the healthy translucency was clouded, the whole egg became dull and dirty. Within a few days Saprolegnia, the fungus that had blinded the dying female, found the dead thing and fastened upon it. At first it was only a spot on the chorion, then it sank roots down into the congealed yolk and grew from them to a coating of mold over the whole egg and from that into white tendrils which reached slowly out to the other eggs of the small cluster. The tendrils slid along, more and more of them, blindly reaching and feeling until they had gripped and laced and twined themselves among the healthy eggs. In the choking grip of the tendrils these eggs died also and the fungus spread until the whole dead cluster was covered with gray mold.

But this was the sum of death in that upstream pocket of the redd while the freshet poured over it. A week or two later the old Senator sat on his burned stump and watched the bottom of the river again. He could see the outlines of the redd quite plainly, because the slight silting had not fully recemented its surface and the brown growth of diatoms had not yet re-established itself on the stones the female had disturbed. But the surface of the redd was more even than it had been before the flood. The partially completed pocket at the upstream end was filled in and the mound of gravel at the lower end had been flattened almost to the level of the stream bed. The old man nodded his head contentedly. He felt that the big female's redd was safe, that her life was perpetuated there under the gravel; and he went home more happily than he had during the flood.

Under the leveled surface of the redd the healthy eggs, Spring's among them, were developing rapidly in the water from autumn-warm earth and rocks. At four weeks they showed the first visible change—two black spots on each egg, disproportionately large yet seeming exactly what they were, the eyes of the embryo. With the appearance of the eye spots the eggs passed from the intermediate period of delicacy and became once more as hardy as they had been at first. As the temperature of the water fell in December development was slower, but the eggs remained clean and healthy in the layer of gravel under the crust of silt. This crust had built up, or rather built down into the redd, to a depth of almost two inches, and while it in some measure reduced the flow of water through the redd it formed a protection against the fungus spores that were always ready to attack dead or injured eggs. By the end of December the embryos were stirring vigorously within the chorions of their eggs and early in January hatching began. The alevins burst forth upon their limited world in strange ways and after varying intensities and lengths of struggle. A few thrust forth heads with staring black eyes and tiny, ineffectual mouths, soon followed by frantically fanning pectoral fins; these hatched slowly and with the greatest expenditure of effort. The great majority hatched tail first and seemed for a brief while reluctant to leave the old security. Spring was among these. Her tail and her whole body up to what would one day be the forward ray of her dorsal fin was suddenly free, moving gently with half a hundred others in the soft flow of water through the redd. In a little while her back broke through, then her head, overburdened with its two great eyes, and finally the shattered chorion dropped away from the yolk of the egg, which was left to form her distended belly.

She was still embryonic, larva rather than fish, and still sustained by the fluid of the yolk, which drew up into her body through a single great vein. Her body was encircled by a continuous transparent fin, perhaps like that of an adult ancestor a million generations back, but quite unlike the fins that she herself would shortly develop. These—dorsal, adipose, caudal, anal, ventral— were indicated by unevennesses in the continuous membrane and by thickening of its transparency; only the pectoral fins, one on either side a little behind her head, gave a real indication of what the development would be. And these had a use, even at that early stage.

Her body was translucent, much of it transparent, revealing vertebrae, ribs, the great artery along her backbone. Life was still less than individual, almost entirely mechanical. Spring's mouth opened and closed, her gills and her pectoral fins moved with it, her body pulsed and her tiny organs did their work. But she was huddled among the other alevins of the central egg-cluster of the pocket and they all obeyed the same rhythm, lying in the gravel, heads upstream, pectoral fins moving steadily, maintaining a flow of good water through gills, along slender bodies.

In this stage they were still hardy as they had been in the stage between the eyeing of the eggs and hatching and they were safer from outside dangers than they would ever again be in their whole lives. Had there been death or injury among them to give it a start the fungus might have choked the healthy alevins and fastened upon them, but it had too recently evolved to its parasitic habit to be able to fasten upon live, healthy flesh; and in that upstream pocket of the redd there was no dead or injured thing except the outlying cluster of eggs that Saprolegnia had already found. There was danger of another flood, but little or no chance that it would have scoured out any part of the redd. The light silting and binding of the surface of the redd that went on through the recurrent small raises of the river during the winter months left the alevins with all the oxygen they needed—their need steadily decreased as development went on and the yolk-sacs grew smaller—and at the same time built up an ever-thicker screen which might have been a sufficient protection from the fungus had any of the alevins died.

Within the redd, at that depth of a foot or more under the surface of the gravel, there were no enemies. And, strangely, there was no creature, bird or mammal or fish, designed to dig down into the redd and find such easy prey as the alevins would have made. Up and down the river there were a thousand potential enemies—mallards, mergansers, goldeneyes, bears, mink and coon, trout and char and bullheads, insects of a hundred different kinds. But they fed on the rotting carcases or broken flesh of the spawned-out salmon and knew nothing of the flesh that still lived within the redds.

Among the horde of alevins Spring developed much as the others did, neither slower nor faster. Her yolk-sac, which had at first been an almost perfect sphere except for the flattening of her body on the upper side, became an irregular oval, widest where it was attached to her body, bulging forward a little under her gills, pinched in slightly towards the lower end, the whole slanting backwards through its pendent length. The surface of the yolk was a tracery of delicate, deep-red veins and was flecked with oil bubbles. Where it grew into her body her liver was plainly visible through the membrane, a strong orange against the paler orange-pink of the rest of the yolk. As the weeks passed the yolk drew up into her body, the single primitive fin evolved slowly into its several parts and she became more and more nearly a fish.

During this time Spring had been growing steadily and she was now almost three-quarters of an inch long. About four weeks after hatching her growth-rate decreased, quite independently of the temperature of the water, and her respiration, the opening and closing of her gills, became slower. This decrease of growth and respiration continued steadily until, five weeks after hatching, she was actually using considerably less oxygen than she had at any time since hatching. Her yolk-sac was less than a third the size it had been when the broken chorion dropped away from it and it was tidy, held tightly up under her in an even swelling from pectoral to ventral fins. These changes in them seemed to make the alevins restless. They began to change position in the pocket and in a little while the strongest of them began to work upwards through the gravel, very slowly, not more than an inch or two a day, but with increasing vigor. Soon they were all scattered through the loose gravel between the solid bed of the river and the surface crust of the redd.

Spring worked up among the others and at this point she felt the first strong urge of her life, became for the first time an individual instead of part of a mass. She wriggled her way slowly through layer after layer of gravel, resting for many hours at a time between each struggle, towards the danger that awaited in the crust of silt at the surface. For the weak among the alevins, struggling too long to break through, or even for the strong that chose a thick or hard place for their attack, there was suffocation in the crust. Yet once again they had a measure of protection. They reached the crust of the redd almost exactly fifteen weeks after the big female had spawned them, when they were within three weeks of complete development. For two or three weeks they had been using less and less oxygen and as they came to the crust they were able to endure conditions that would have killed them a short while before. They attacked the crust with tiny urgency, burrowing into it, drawing back to rest and breathe in the current of their fanning pectoral fins, stirring the silt in gray-brown clouds around them so that it dropped down among the clean stones of the redd. Spring, struggling in the darkness, driven by a first sensation of fear, came suddenly into strong light. She turned quickly from it to hide among the stones on the surface of the redd.

For the next three weeks she moved little in her hiding place among the stones, but in that time she began to feed, although she was still drawing the fluid from her yolk-sac. Down in the body of the redd the alevins had lived in almost complete separation from the rest of life, under more nearly aseptic conditions than those of a modern hospital nursery. On the surface of the redd there was life all about them and they drew it into their mouths and fed upon it almost in the act of breathing. It was March when they first reached the surface of the redd and there was a brown growth of diatoms on the stones and boulders of the stream. Colonies of Meridion making hollow-centered discs, of Asterionella grouped like the spokes of a wagon wheel, microscopic themselves but gathering yet smaller food and so rendering it to the larger plankton forms that fed on them, were rendered in turn through the plankton to the insects and through these again to the fish. But Spring was still something less than fish and the first food that she took from the water about her was Meridion and Asterionella, individuals broken from their colonies and drifting down to her with the stream. She did not reach out for these and swallow them; they were strained from the water she breathed by tiny rake-teeth on her gill arches and slipped from there down into her body with the closing of her gills. From these it was a natural advance to the organic planktons when they came to her, the flagellates and rotifers and crustaceans, even to great Daphnia, washed down from the lakes and plainly visible to the human eye as an active, reddish speck.

Two weeks after she had broken through the crust of the redd the last outward sign of Spring's yolk-sac had disappeared and the walls of her abdominal cavity closed over it. It was there and serving her still for almost a week longer and through that week she still clung to darkness under the stones. At the end of the eighteenth week after her egg had dropped from the big female she accepted light, lying in the eddy behind one of the larger stones on the bottom. She was free-swimming fry, fish at last, and subject to the laws of hunger that governed the whole life of the river except at spawning time. In her eddy behind the stone more food came to her, and gradually she began to reach out for it instead of straining it from the water she breathed. Pursuing food she swam out of her eddy into the full force of the current. It threw her off balance, swept her a few inches downstream before she could recover and find shelter behind another stone. She tried again and again was unbalanced. But by the third time her tiny fins were doing their work, holding her, balancing her, planing her; she intercepted the daphne that had drawn her, turned like a full-grown fish and regained the shelter of the stone she had left.

From the burnt stump on the bank of the pool the old Senator saw the flash of her turn. Occasionally his quick eye caught other tiny flashes across the tail of the pool and he knew that the salmon were hatched. "I have seen the thing through so far this time," he told himself, "that there is almost nothing more that a man can see of it. Yet I have lived by the river for better than fifty years and not seen it before. I could have used it when I was younger, but there isn't time then to see things properly." He picked up his rod and walked up to the head of the pool. Standing on the rock near the wall of the canyon he began to cast a big fly well across the pool, working it back, slow and deep, towards his own bank. He moved down gradually, covering the water carefully, and the fly swam lazily near the bottom, almost touching the stone behind which Spring was lying. The shape of a great fish passed over Spring, following the fly. It turned sharply, with a flash that lighted the whole pool, and ran swiftly downstream. Spring hid from it, as deeply as she could work her way down among the stones.

## CHAPTER FOUR

SPRING fed more and more actively as she grew stronger. The April sun warmed the water and stirred life from among the rocks and stones of the river bed. Many small things were brought directly to her as she held in the current or sheltered from it behind a stone on the bottom, but very often she swam out and intercepted food that was being carried past to right or left of her. After such excursions she did not always return to her original place, and little by little, because the current at the side of the pool was slower and held more feed, she was drawn towards the bank. It was an unfelt migration; she made little darts and drives both to right and left of her, but for every dart to the right she made two or three to the left because there was more food there and it was more easily caught. In the same way and at the same time she worked her way a few feet upstream of where she had first broken through the gravel. And so, in the second or third week of April, she found herself in the big eddy at the side of the pool, behind the rock wall at the mouth of the canyon.

A good proportion of the little fish hatched from the same redd had worked across to the eddy in much the same way, but already the process of cutting down the ten thousand eggs of the big female to the two fish that would one day return to spawn and fertilize ten thousand more eggs had begun. A few had died as alevins in breaking through the crust, but nearly all had lived to absorb the yolk-sac and begin feeding freely. Then, because they no longer hid closely among the uneven stones of the bottom, they became exposed to their enemies. They fed and moved in the open water because they had to and because they had no fear of the thing that might happen, only of the thing that was happening. So the birds found them and the fish found them and even the insects, the great fierce dragonfly nymphs with their hooked and grasping underjaws, found some of them. The losses began slowly and gradually and went on slowly and gradually, as they would through all the freshwater life and the saltwater years,

right up until the unwasted deaths of the few that returned to spawn.

Early migration, too, drew the young chinooks from
the pool. Many of the tens of thousands that broke
through the surface of their redds in the fantail during
March, drawn by their inheritance or by some mechanical force, had started their journey down the long
reaches to the sea before the middle of April. Spring
and the others that remained in the pool were held there
in the same way—perhaps because some inclination to remain longer in fresh water had entered into them from
the body of the big female, perhaps because they found
in the eddy food and conditions to their liking.

Looking down at Spring's eddy one might not have
suspected that there was much in it for her to feed on.
It was a large eddy, fully a hundred feet long and forming the rough segment of a circle, perhaps thirty feet
wide at its widest point, with the shore-line as the arc.
The bottom, sloping gradually from deep water where
the reversing current of the eddy touched the main
flow of the river, was of water-worn boulders, gray and
brown and green, some of them two or three feet in
diameter, many smaller, all rounded under their algal
growth and encrustations. For Spring, when her attention was not too closely drawn by mayfly nymph or
chironomid larva, it had a different appearance. The
greens and browns of the rocks below her were faith-
fully reflected in the smooth underface of the water
except only in a circle of light immediately above her,

a circle that varied in diameter as she was higher or lower in the water, narrowest when she was close under the surface, widest when she was down among the rocks of the bottom. Because the branched green alga, Cladophora, was the dominant growth on the rocks at the bottom of the eddy, creatures moving or swimming in Spring's world were also green to her even when they passed directly over her through the circular window of clear light. Unless they were deeper in the water than herself, it was only when they passed into the window or its widening projection above the surface of the water that she could see clearly the enemies, birds, fish or mammals, which threatened her, or the smaller creatures that she herself threatened.

Life in the eddy was fast, competitive, nearly always dangerous. Most of the young chinooks held themselves in midwater near the outer edge of the eddy, where the two currents passed each other, and their bodies moved constantly in quick, sinuous rhythm that fluttered their tail fins. They were moving swiftly and almost constantly from side to side or up and down in the water, seizing in their jaws any tiny thing within reach, often ejecting it again as soon as it was seized. They were learning, and learning slowly, what was useful to them and what was not. In the fierce rush of competition they dared not select lest something might be lost to them in the hesitation.

Spring, moved by her enemies as well as in search for food, traveled through most of the eddy in time. The mergansers, dipping their heads under the water, diving, hunting small fish and insects, came often to the pool at the foot of the canyon. They sat on the rocks at the edge of the water for half an hour or an hour at a time, then slid from these to fish. Spring was aware of them usually through sharp disturbance of the smooth flow of life in the eddy and at such times she sank down to the bottom to lie motionless and almost invisible among the boulders. Green shapes, dimly seen in midwater, feathers flashing like schools of tiny fish as the shapes turned, held her there until the danger was past. Once she saw nothing until a saw-toothed bill and narrow head swam suddenly into the edge of the circle of clear light directly above her. The body, still outside the circle and reflecting the green of the bottom, was almost invisible. The legs and webbed feet, moving gently, green and themselves reflected again in the mirror underface of the water, did little to warn. It was the head, dark against the sky, with a suggestion of the rusty red plumage around the darkness, that forced itself upon Spring's quick eye and drove her down for safety. The merganser caught the flash of her downward flight and dived. Spring's vigorous inch and a half of body drove down towards a crevice among the rocks; almost in safety she saw the great mouth and spiny fins of a bullhead, a creature of terror fully twice as long as herself, immediately before her. She turned from it, the bullhead pursued. The merganser, drawn by the flash of Spring's turning, came full upon the flash of the bullhead's pursuit. She drove after it, seized it across the body just behind the head, and turned back to the surface. Spring ran on, turning and twisting in panic, sending from her bright body the little flashes that would have guided her enemy unerringly after her but for the bullhead's intervention. In shallow water near the shore of the eddy she ran out of her panic and found her way down among the rocks, to wait in the safety of stillness until the pool seemed calm again.

She had no time, in that busy competitive life, to remain long inactive, and very soon the memory of danger was no longer with her. Even so her return to activity was gradual. From a motionless olive-green stick, tightly pressed between two protecting rocks, she became a fish again; her dorsal fin rose to its erect position, her tail spread itself and almost without seeming to have moved she was once more poised on her pectoral and ventral fins, alert and ready to feed. Some tiny thing in the water caught her attention. She opened her mouth, seized it, chewed, expelled it with a rush of water. Her tail fin was moving again now and the fins beneath her seemed to vibrate. She took something else, ejected it. A mayfly nymph, starting its journey towards the surface, moved in front of her. She swam to it quickly, seized it and swallowed it. A moment later she had found a tiny midge larva in its soft olive-brown tube and swallowed that also. She turned and moved a little towards the shore. There was something round and big in front of her, seemingly suspended a few inches above the bottom of the eddy. She swam towards it and was faced suddenly by a fish smaller than herself, a bristling fierce little fish with bright red throat and rotund belly. Spring hesitated, turned from him, felt a fierce blow on her side and fled. The stickleback remained perfectly still in the water for a moment, his pectorals spread, then turned in two or three jerky movements, darted back and stopped abruptly beside his nest. Striking Spring he had missed his stroke. Driving under her he might have ripped her belly with the sharp spines of his back.

Spring's flight took her back to the deeper part of the eddy where the upstream current flowed more strongly, carrying with it small things drawn from the edge of the main current—larvae of midges and gnats, danceflies, blackflies and beetles. As the month drew on there were more and more winged creatures to be taken on the surface and the young salmon began to watch and wait for them. Spring spent much time in the very edge of the main current, holding herself in place with quick unceasing movement of body and tail fin, poised and ready to move swiftly in any direction, up or down, to right or left, for food. She learned to watch for the mayflies to float into her circle of clear light at the surface—first the tips of the upright gauzy wings breaking the edge of the circle, then the whole wings and the body, the six feet dimpling the surface and the two or three long tail-whisks. At such moments the beat of her body-movement speeded, she seemed stretched and taut on quick fins. As the fly came towards her she would move up to meet it, body straining, mouth open, finally breaking the surface in a hurried dash to seize or miss the so-desired thing and swim swiftly back to her position. All about her the little salmon rose to anything that was food and much that was not food at all. The trout, rainbows and cutthroats, some large, some small, fed amongst them more deliberately, taking mayflies and chironomids and stoneflies with easy calm, bothering the small fish seldom or not at all because they were strong, quick difficult prey. But if one were injured or sick, betraying its condition by the flash of its unbalanced body, a trout would drive instantly upon it, following the flashes of its crippled flight relentlessly to seize and swallow it.

One morning early in May, Spring was feeding more deeply in the water than usual. The blackflies and chironomids were rising to the surface to break out wings, and all the salmon and trout of the eddy were busily intercepting them. In the downstream edge of her circle of light Spring was dimly aware that something moved, but it was a distant thing, not clear to her against the muddled dark background of second-growth fir trees that rimmed her circle on that side, and she cared nothing for it. Behind her the large trout stopped feeding and sank down among the boulders. Above them small fish went on feeding, moving freely and quickly in the water, grabbing, swallowing, ejecting, their slender bodies and tail fins busy.

From the bank Senator Evans and Don Gunner looked down into the eddy. "It's a lovely pool," Gunner said. "No wonder you come up here so often."

The old man smiled. "I like it," he said simply. "And you've helped me understand it a little."

Gunner shook his head. "Not I," he said. "I often think you old anglers come much closer to understanding a place like this than scientists do. You may not be able to name all the whys and wherefores, but you understand without that. You feel it."

"There's something in that, all right. One does get the feel of a piece of water, fishing over it and watching it. But there's a word you moderns use a whole lot—rhythm. And that's what you've taught me, the rhythms of life in small places like this, even if I can't grasp them in the wider places." The old man's voice dropped a little almost as though he were alone and speaking to himself. "From algae to plankton to insects to fish, from diatom to daphne to stonefly to fish again. From there to the birds and animals, finally man. And it all starts from decay, chemicals, bacteria. And goes back there. I like it," he said again, and Gunner could feel the strength that the thing had for him.

Down in the eddy the little fish were still feeding and it was easy to watch them in the good light. "What are they?" Evans asked.

"Trout fry, a lot of them. But there are plenty of chinooks too, I'm sure of that."

"Fish spending their whole first year in fresh water?"

"Most of them, I guess. This stream is quite a bit above sea-level and all of three hundred miles from the mouth of the Columbia, so it's likely to have a good proportion of stream-type fish."

"About what proportion? Fifty per cent? Seventy-five?"

Gunner shook his head. "Shouldn't think it would be that much. Working on fish out in salt water you generally get about twenty-two per cent stream-type and the rest ocean-type. Most of the stream-type fish belong to the spring run, which comes to streams like this, a long way back from salt water. But even so I doubt if you'd get fifty per cent stream-type from here."

Senator Evans looked hard at the little fish in the eddy. He was thinking of the big female, wondering if any of them might have come from her eggs. He felt that he wanted to know more about them, if possible somehow to make them his own. "Don," he said suddenly. "Couldn't I mark some of these fish?"

"Sure you could. It's not a very good place for a trap, but you could get a few."

"I wouldn't need a trap if there was a decent hatch of mayflies. They feed on the surface as freely as brown trout and they'll take anything. But how could I mark them?"

"Use a good sharp pair of nail clippers and take the adipose fin and the left ventral right off at the base. That's the combination they are using for this stream in this year's experiment. Of course you wouldn't be

49

able to tell them from the ones Shorey's marking down below, but if you see any adults this far up you'll be pretty safe in telling yourself they're your fish."

"Couldn't I use a different combination?"

Gunner shook his head. "It might make some confusion. You see they allot all the combinations at the beginning of the year, so as to keep the experiments separate. If they picked up your fish down in the Willamette or somewhere in the lower reaches of the Columbia with the wrong mark on them it might throw out somebody's figures. If you use Shorey's mark you can tell him how many fish you've released and it won't matter to anyone. I'll mention it to him tonight."

The two men talked a little while longer, then turned away from the pool and went off down the trail towards the Senator's house. Spring was not even aware that their heads were no longer visible against the rim of her circle of light. She had been feeding steadily for nearly two hours and for the first time in her free-swimming life she was almost gorged. She hung lazily in the water, taking only such food as floated almost into her mouth. Lying quietly she seemed bigger than she really was and the markings and colors of her body were very clear. Her back was a dark olive color, spotted with black. Along each side of her were nine heavy parr-marks, like fingerprints, and the black spots on her back spread down among them, below the lateral line and almost to her belly. Her belly was silver, shading to a brassy color on the lower part of her sides and from this through varying olives to the dark of her back. Her fins were pale red, in sharp contrast to the brilliant orange fins of the few young silver salmon in the pool. Her tail was noticeably forked and her head was small but large-eyed still. By the end of May she was about two and a half inches long. The scales protecting her whole body, unformed when she had become free-swimming two months before, now marked the progress of her growth through those months by six or seven concentric rings added to each of the tiny discs that had first formed.

## CHAPTER FIVE

DURING May the turnover of life in the eddy, keeping pace with the rising temperature of the stream, had grown faster and faster. June and July were the peak months of plenty, with the temperature rising steadily through the high fifties and up into the sixties in spite of an abundant flow of water from melting snow in the hills. The green algae of the eddy, drawing energy from the sunlight and feeding vigorously on the dissolved minerals of the river water, grew thickly everywhere. A few trailing stems of the river weed, Potamogeton, moved gently in the slacker current near shore. The diatoms, Asterionella and many others replacing the earlier abundance of Meridion, multiplied. Minute green desmids, each with its exactly bisecting band of transparency, grew rapidly; every night thousands upon thousands of them split across their transparent bands, each into two separate individuals which already showed the transparency from which they in turn would multiply.

Amongst these and upon these other life lived and fed. Diatoms formed a coat of brownish slime on the stems and leaves of Potamogeton, as they did on the round boulders of the bottom, and in this were rotifers and tiny moss plants and the jellied egg-sacs of larger creatures such as snails and midges. In all there was constant change, death and new life, freshness and decay, cycles within cycles. From it and matching it stemmed the larger life of insects and molluscs, worms and leeches and crustaceans. From these grew Spring's life and the lives of the larger fish of the eddy.

Spring had chosen herself a place that she seldom left, above a larger brown boulder at the lower end of the eddy and near the outer edge. She held here hour after hour, facing downstream into the returning current, feeding. She still took into her jaws many things that she rejected almost immediately, but the abundance of useful things was so great that she fed without difficulty. Up in the sharp rapid above the Canyon Pool a blackfly larva, clinging to the crown of a boulder in full rush of fast water, sought to change its position. Held fast to the boulder by the sucking disc in its tail, head downstream and its feeding fans spread out on either side to strain small feed from the current, it dropped a thread from its mouth to the boulder. Almost at once the sucking disc released its hold and the larva was swept down to hang from the thread. Its body bent and twisted until the disc found a new hold, then the thread was released and it was once more with its head downstream, more than twice its own length from where it had started. The movement was repeated several times. Then suddenly, as with a human climber on a rock face, there was a slip, some failure of the technique. The larva swept down with the current into the pool, its body twisting and wriggling, sucking disc and thread seeking a hold. Still in the edge of the main current it was swept down the length of the eddy, caught for a moment in the vortex and carried back to where Spring was waiting. She took it almost quietly and swallowed it, a quarter-inch of succulence.

Below her, on the brown boulder and beneath it, things moved. Almost buried in a patch of sand on the downstream side a large dragonfly nymph waited, watching the clumsy movement of a caddis grub. The caddis grub, cowlike and heavy, browsed with its fellows among the diatoms and algae of the rock, working steadily down towards the waiting nymph. In a clump of moss it came upon a chironomid larva, reached out eager forelegs and seized it. The effort dislodged the grip of its four remaining claw-tipped legs and it fell from the rock, still gripping the chironomid. It lay on its back, struggling to right itself without losing its prey, nearly an inch away from the motionless dragon nymph. There was a flicker of something between the two insects and the dragon nymph had reached out its long, grasping lower jaw and seized the caddis. It shifted position, stirring the sand in a little cloud. The caddis, feeling the grip of the two curving hooks of the dragon's lower jaw, had dropped the chironomid and drawn its head and legs back into its case. By this time it was within reach of the dragon nymph's mouth and the grip tightened, piercing the protection of the case, pressing the thin-skinned white body inside. The caddis grub's head and six legs, black and shining, came out of the case again, struggling violently to find a grip of anything at all. The head turned back to the dragon nymph, biting. But it was an unequal struggle. The rear half of the case, bitten through, fell to the sand. The caddis, still holding fast to the remains with its caudal hooks, lay for a moment free, white body undulating with the movement that had served all through its life to make a flow of water through its case, tufted abdominal gills, almost like the legs of a caterpillar, working. Then the dragon nymph moved sharply forward, seized it again and began its meal.

The struggle had disturbed Callibeatis, a slender mayfly nymph with the pepper-and-salt transparency of a shrimp. She was about a half-inch long, dainty and fragile, yet quick and active. Like the caddis and the dragon nymph she had six legs, each with a tiny claw at the end of it. Along each side of her body was a series of seven gill plates that had been legs some billions of generations before, and her three tails were fringed with tiny hairs. She swam through the water with a fishlike movement of tail and body and rapid beat of her gill plates, to cling to the overhang of the boulder. The dragon nymph, moving as it fed on the still-struggling caddis, disturbed her again. She swam upwards swiftly. Spring saw her and caught her. A moment later another nymph, swimming upwards to shed its skin at the surface and fly away as a dun, passed too close to Spring and was caught.

There was life also on the under side of the brown rock, where it rested on the gravel and silt. Near the outer edge where the current flowed past, the Hydropsyche caddis sheltered in a case of pebbles built on to the rock and spun out a funnel-shaped net to catch tiny food. Farther under were black, flattened mayfly nymphs and more caddis grubs with cases of wood or grains of sand. Many of these had grown to full size, casting off the hind-ends of their cases as they grew and building on to the wider forward end, and were passing through the brief pupal stage, quiescent in partially sealed cases save for the body-movement that still drew water past them. A small leech, bearing its young under its belly, passed with a gliding movement between two stationary caddis cases. Stonefly nymphs, large, two-tailed and with double grappling claws on the end of each strong, jointed leg moved easily and confidently. They were hunting midge larvae and mayfly nymphs and other smaller creatures than these, though little mayfly nymphs rode securely on the backs of several. Nearly all that were still under the brown rock in June had spent two years in the eddy since hatching; in a little while they would crawl out of the water on to rocks or twigs to cast their nymphal shucks and fly away. The movement would expose them to Spring's attack. Yet two or three months earlier they, as well as the dragon nymph, might have made her their prey.

Though Spring found the bulk of her food in midwater during the months of plenty, there was much on the surface to draw her. Aphids, leaf-hoppers, ants, bees, even a grasshopper, were carried to her in the returning current of the eddy and as each came into her circular window of light she rose eagerly to meet it. But the true abundance of the river was on the bottom, among the rocks and in the silt, on the trailing stems of Potamogeton and among the debris of rotting wood along the shore of the eddy. Here it was in large measure safe from her and from most of the other midwater foragers until some accident of current or the close pattern of its life cycle forced it away from protection. It was the turnover of life rather than the store of life in the river upon which Spring and the other fish lived and grew fat, and in the hot summer months the pace of the turnover was tremendous. Daphnia, scarcely a week or two out of the egg, would herself be carrying a brood of eggs, to shed them and ripen others for shedding in the space of a few days. Some of the rotifers, having a life span of little more than two weeks, began laying eggs on the third day and kept busily at it until caught in the nets of Hydropsyche or until they sank to the bottom exhausted and dying. Callibeatis, mature at the beginning of April, laid a thousand eggs; by the middle of May the survivors of her brood were themselves mature, spent and dying upon the surface of the water after laying their own thousands of eggs. By the end of June Spring was catching the full-grown nymphs of the third generation as they rose through the water to moult their skins.

On a June evening the sedges were thick over the water. Spring had attacked them a day or two earlier, when, as caddis pupae, they were biting through their sealed cases and ascending to the surface of the water. Now they hovered and fluttered in hundreds above the eddy, softly brown and mothlike. Their brief term of aerial existence was almost over. Mouthless, unable to feed after breaking from the pupal case, they had hastened to mate and lay their eggs. Now they carried themselves heavily on tiring wings, falling at last to the surface of the water to rest themselves into death. Spring and the other fish of the eddy hung near the surface to feed on them as they floated in the current. Spring still rose eagerly and clumsily, but she took many and they were, for her, heavy feeding. Among them chironomids, tiny true midges with slender black bodies, plumed antennae and pale smoky wings, danced in regimented clouds, rising and falling together in mechanically perfect formation. Many of these also were on the surface of the eddy and Spring fed steadily until the full moon was bright in the sky.

From downstream a small dark mink, bright-eyed in the moonlight, came questing along the rocks at the edge of the river. He ran quickly, his body humped, but stopped very often to stand almost straight up, his forepaws on the top of a boulder, and look about him. Along the shore of the eddy he stopped twice, but he went on each time and it seemed that he meant to follow the river up into the canyon. He stopped again, raising his head very high, dilating his damp nostrils until his long whiskers seemed to quiver. Then he turned sharply, ran back along the shore, stopped again. He raised himself briefly, looked once at the bank behind him, then slipped forward into the water. He swam very softly, streaking the surface of the eddy only a little in the moonlight. Then suddenly the silver ripples stopped and he was gone, leaving only a faint dark swirl that scarcely spread beyond its start.

Spring was suddenly aware of disturbance in the eddy. A flash of moonlight, reflected from the wet hairs of the sharply twisting mink, reached her as she turned down towards the rocks below. But the mink had already selected a small trout for himself and he followed its every move, turning and twisting until he was close upon its flight. He caught it near the bottom and returned to the shore of the eddy to make his meal. He fished again in the pool that night and Spring, her belly full from earlier feeding, held down among the protecting boulders until the sunlight was strong on the pool.

In the morning the mayflies were almost as abundant as the sedges had been the evening before. Spring was drawn by easy stages to her station above the brown rock. A nymph came from behind the rock, she saw it and did not move. Another came, she tried for it and missed, but stayed in midwater. A chironomid came up from the bottom, she caught it and swallowed it. The current brought a tiny clump of algae, close under the surface. She came up to it, took it in her jaws, spat it out. But once again she remained where the pursuit had taken her, fluttering her tail to hold her three-inch length within easy reach of the surface. This was before the mayflies began to come thickly and for a while she fed chiefly on chironomids. But all through the eddy and in the pool itself and in the rapids above the pool mayfly nymphs were stirring and in a little while they were moving up through the water. At the surface they split their nymphal skins and emerged, slim-bodied and with upright wings, to float down a little way, then fly. At first Spring was taking them a little below the surface. Then they began to come to her on the surface, often rising from it just as she swam up to seize them. The light nymphal shucks collected in numbers along the edge of the eddy and Spring rose to many of these also. Then for a short while there was a pause.

As they rose from the water into their first flight the mayflies were still not perfect adults. They flew away to the land, to light on alder leaves and fir needles, on wild currant bushes, on salal, even on the ground. Resting there they cast yet another skin, a rough transparent veil that covered body and wings and tails. As this left them they became polished and brilliant, yet unbelievably fragile and graceful. Soon they flew again, and in a little while they were over the water again, many hundreds of them over the big pool and the eddy, fluttering up and down almost as the sedges had the evening before, in smooth and rhythmic flight. The sunlight decorated their perfection of form and color. A few dipped to the water and rested there briefly, poised on six delicate legs, their three long tails held up from the water, transparent, intricately veined wings upright like tiny sails, body colors fresh and glistening, the whole reflected in the smooth surface of the water. But they rested briefly if at all, for this was the mating flight, the final purpose of their lives, and the time for it was short. For a while longer they danced in the sun above the water, females dipping often to drop their eggs. Spring still hung near the surface and occasionally something came to her. Then the mayflies began to drop to the water, at first a few, then more and more. Some of them, utterly exhausted in mid-flight, dropped almost abruptly and collapsed at once with flattened wings. Others lighted, rose again, flew a little upstream, lighted again. For a few yards they floated with wings proudly upright, then quietly and wearily they let them fall to the water, at right angles to their bodies. And life had gone from many even as the wing muscles relaxed.

Spring fed busily in her chosen place, but she did not hold it for very long after the mayflies began to drop back to the water. She became aware of a big trout behind her, feeding lazily, moving slowly forward. Almost imperceptibly she edged in towards the shore of the eddy, not more than a foot or two but away from the brown stone that marked her holt. The big trout moved up over the stone. In a little while she was back near his tail, perhaps six inches away from it, towards the shore. The trout fed busily enough but mayflies passed him and Spring took many.

As she fed a quick shadow flicked the edge of her circular window of light two or three times. On the bank Senator Evans, kneeling, dried his fly and marked the rise of the big trout lying ahead of Spring. Twice more he flicked the false casts out over the water, then shot the tiny fly and let it touch the surface six inches ahead of the big fish and a little to one side of him. His fly was dainty, resting on sparse gleaming hackles, with outspread wings and three tails drooping even as those of the spent mayflies. The trout moved away from it to take another fly, turned back towards it and found yet another fly had lighted almost on top of him. He took it with surprised clumsiness and the

Senator's fly drifted down along his length to where Spring was waiting. Spring rose and took it gladly.

The old man moved not at all, hoping that she would spit out the fly and let him recover it quietly. For some reason, perhaps because she sensed that all was not well with the fly, Spring turned sharply down towards the shelter of the bottom. She drew the light gut after her, still holding the fly, then came sharply against the drag of the greased and floating line. The sudden pull set the sharp point of the small hook firmly in her jaw. The old man saw his floating line go down and began to recover it gently through the rings of his rod. Spring struggled and drove for the bottom, but she was pulled off balance, dragged away from safety. She turned and swam swiftly upwards in the direction of the pull, jumped clear of the water, fell over herself, jumped again and was held close to the bank, resting quietly on her side. The old man took the gut in his hand and looked down at her.

"Heavy parr-marks," he said a little uncertainly, as though doubting his power to apply the mystic identification formula Gunner had given him. "Pale fins and the last ray of the anal short. Chinook, all right." He still felt that he would have liked to have Gunner at his elbow to confirm the opinion, but he fumbled in his pocket and brought out a small pair of clippers. Very carefully he lifted Spring from the water. Holding her firmly, but with a slow, almost an awed gentleness, he clipped off the little fatty fin above her tail, turned her in his hand and clipped away the left ventral. Then he freed the hook and set her back in the water.

Spring lay for a moment in the cup of the old man's hand, gulping water through her gills. Then her panic returned and she swam off, a little queerly, towards the bottom. She found a place between two stones, not far from the brown boulder, and lay there, still as a stick, her head in the shade. Above her the old Senator's false casts flicked out again, gradually lengthening. The fly fell softly once more above the big trout. He moved over to it, sucked it in gently, turned back. The old man moved, the line tightened, the trout plunged away from the pull. For five full minutes the trout fought, sending the bright flashes of its body all through the pool, running, leaping to fall back and crush half-a-dozen dying mayflies under the surface at each leap. The old man humored him, let him go, held him, drew him at last gently over his waiting net. Spring knew nothing of all this.

## CHAPTER SIX

FOR two or three days after her release Spring's movements were awkward and uncertain and she fed scarcely at all, though the flow of plenty through the water about her and on the surface above her never ceased. The loss of her adipose fin affected her not at

63

all—the little fin was nothing more than a degenerate survival from some earlier stage of evolution and served no useful purpose. But she had to readjust her whole body to the loss of the one ventral fin, and the short journey from the old Senator's hand to the shelter of the rocks on the bottom had been enough to destroy her easy confidence in her power of movement through the water. The exact balance that held her evenly poised in the water at all times was destroyed; and her power of quick and certain movement up or down was impaired.

From time to time in the first few days she made small tentative movements from her hiding place, but always sank back again when she found that her body did not respond to the movement of her muscles as she had learned to expect it to. The cautious process of adjustment, insensibly passed through close to the shelter of the bottom, almost certainly saved her life. In midwater the flashes of her unbalanced body would have drawn the pursuit of trout or merganser, perhaps even of a chinook fingerling little larger than herself. When she raised herself from the bottom down there among the rounded boulders what slight flash there was passed but a little distance from her.

By the third or fourth day she was feeding busily, though still without moving far from shelter. From that point her adjustment was rapid and in less than a week her movements were almost as sure and quick as they had ever been. By the end of the second week she was back in her position over the brown rock, feeding at the surface or in midwater as freely as she had on the morning of the great hatch of mayflies. Only in the missing fins and, later, on the concentric rings of her rapidly growing scales, was there any clear sign that she had once been handled by a human being. About ten rings from the center of each scale there formed a group of two or three rings very closely spaced, making a dark ridge that showed the check in her growth.

The abundance of food in the eddy increased and persisted through July, and rose to its peak in August. Spring took for herself everything that came near her and seemed small enough—nymphs of mayflies and stoneflies, larvae of blackflies and midges and gnats, netwings, danceflies and beetles. Many of these she found also at the surface as winged creatures and with them there came to her land insects, ants and leaf bugs, sometimes honey bees and yellowjackets and common flies. The dangers and disturbances of those months were comparatively few. The big trout of the pool grew lazy as the hot sun warmed the water of the river. They fed easily at certain times on the plentiful insects, but for long hours of each day they lay close to the bottom or moved slowly about near the tail of the pool, where the smooth flow of water drew out and down into the rapid below. Spring seldom had to yield her position over the brown boulder, though she usually sank well down in the water in the middle of

the day, while the hot sun glared down on the un-
creased surface of the eddy.

Senator Evans came to the pool very often in August
and September, sometimes to fish but generally just to
watch. He liked to be out in the dry weather and the
hot sun, to be able to lie near the pool in the shade
of the rock face of the canyon, reading a book and
glancing up from it often towards the pool or the
banks of the river downstream of where he lay.

His favorite position under the shade of the rock
face was a particularly good one. With the afternoon
sun behind him he could see right down to the bottom
of most parts of the pool and the eddy, and while he
was well above the level of the water his movements
were little noticeable against the background of gray
rock. He liked to be there for the peace and beauty
of the place as well as for what he saw in the water.
To see some little thing clearly, perhaps a trout turning on its side to scrape the Hydropsyche caddis grubs
from the boulders, or a dragon nymph climbing on to
the rock to split and cast its shuck, then spread its
veined and gleaming wings to harden in the sunlight,
was enough, a stored delight to be remembered again
and again, perhaps for many years. He did not expect
to see the big and spectacular things, though these also
sometimes came to him. Once the otters came to the
pool in broad daylight, swimming easily up the rapid
to fish and play in the pool for fully an hour before
they knew they were watched. It was a big thing too

when the old man found that he could quite often distinguish among the other small fish of the pool some of the forty or fifty young chinooks he had caught and marked, and a bigger thing still when he discovered his marks on Spring and realized that she was nearly always to be found in position above the brown boulder.

He sat watching her one day late in September. The sun was still strong and warm, but the water of the river had cooled, the turnover of life was no longer so rapid, food was far less plentiful than it had been the month before. Spring was in midwater over the brown boulder, taking whatever passed near enough to her. Soon a large trout moved up and she edged out of position, towards the bank of the river. Senator Evans, intent upon both fish, was almost startled into movement by the heron's sudden arrival. The heron had come straight upstream, purposefully, knowing exactly what place he sought. His quick suspicious eyes had altogether failed to distinguish the man's shape against the gray rock face. The Senator did not move but he lifted his watching slowly from the water to where the heron was standing near the edge of the eddy. The heron wrapped his great, curved, gray-blue wings about him and seemed quite unconcerned with the water in front of him. He settled himself, gazing sternly across the river, his long neck stretched. Then he turned his head to look downstream, turned it again to look past the Senator up into the canyon. Nothing he saw disturbed him and he raised one leg from the rocks in a movement so slow and so smooth that the old man, watching closely, felt that he was aware of it only by the effect. The long leg and gawky foot came down into the water and the bird shifted his weight. His head was held forward now, the sharp point of his long, broad-based beak held steadily within a few inches of the surface of the water, his folded wings like hunched shoulders. He shifted his weight and stepped forward again, moving with the same imperceptible slowness, sending not the least ripple ahead of him across the glassy surface of the eddy.

The heron waded out until he was standing in more than a foot of water. There he was perfectly still. Senator Evans looked back to where he had last seen Spring, moving his eyes with a slow stealth that matched the heron's. At first he could not see her, but soon he found her eager five-inch length well in towards the shore of the eddy. Spring was more restless than usual. The lowering temperature of the water, the greater scarcity of food, the shorter hours of daylight all worked upon each other and contributed to her restlessness. Combining with these, perhaps in large measure growing out of them, were the first stirrings of the greater restlessness that would draw her on her seaward migration. Now these changes led her farther from the brown rock than she usually moved when yielding place to a larger fish. Instead of easing away a few inches and dropping back well behind the eye of the trout, to wait there and take what came to her, she was working gradually towards the shore of the eddy and the waiting heron. Senator Evans watched her, then glanced back to the heron, gauging the distance between his great beak and her body. She was still well out of reach. Evans did not look back to her again. The heron was motionless, intent upon the water. His stillness and concentration made it difficult to believe that he was breathing, that somewhere under the gray feathers a heart was beating, blood was flowing, change and movement of all kinds were taking place.

The stillness broke from him sharply. His great beak drove down, for a second his head was below the water. Head and beak came up again and the Senator could see the little fish clearly—short tapering body and wide head of a cottoid. Holding it in his beak the heron looked calmly to both sides of him. Then he stretched his neck, pointed his bill upward and swallowed the bullhead. The Senator watched its passage down the long throat, saw the bird shake his feathers as though to ease it past a difficult place. Then the heron was back in his hunched position, his beak close to the water and ready to strike again.

Spring was unaware of what had happened. The ripples from the heron's sharp thrust had scarcely disturbed the water above her. She had seen no movement and she continued to work gradually into danger. Two scaly sticks rose straight from the bottom inshore of her and were reflected again in the mirror of the undersurface. But there was nothing about them to thrust itself upon her awareness; even had they seemed out of place they would not have warned her for they were still, perfectly still, and in stillness there was no danger. Even when she had moved over far enough for the heron's head and the upper part of his folded wings to come within the circle of light above her she still saw nothing that threatened her. The bird's pale head matched the pale light of the sky, and the darker markings, from which grew his long plumes in the breeding season, matched the dark blur of tree tops against the sky. Spring moved in, the bird's fierce eyes upon her.

Senator Evans watched. In some measure it was an affair between the bird and the fish. Spring was one of his marked fish. But she had a thousand such dangers to face before she could return to the pool to spawn. She would survive or not survive and to give her life once might be little enough gain. It was interesting to watch, to have followed it through its series of chances—the movement of the trout, Spring's unusual restlessness, the chance that had held her beyond range of the disturbance of the bullhead's fate. Yet Spring was a special fish, not merely one that he had marked but one that he had watched many times since the marking. She was completely deceived, utterly unconscious of danger. Perhaps the heron deserved the reward of his skill. Yet the heron also was deceived,

utterly unconscious of danger. The elementary justice
of the comparison pleased the old man. Spring was
within reach of the heron's thrust. Evans raised his
hand and pulled a white handkerchief from his pocket.
The heron's head and neck straightened sharply, his
great wings, already spread, beat air and water and
lifted him clumsily. He croaked harshly two or three
times as he rose and flew heavily off downstream.

The Senator watched him out of sight, then looked
back to the water. Spring was down among the rocks
on the bottom and he could not see her. The trout too
had sunk well down in the water and seemed heavy
and dull, no longer poised upon expectant fins. The
old man's attention was drawn by a sudden flurry of
water at the lip of the pool. It was closely followed by
two others. Soon they came up into the main body of
the pool, three spawning chinooks, the first of the
run to come through to this last spawning pool. He
watched them as they swam and circled in the quiet
water, grouping together, a little uncertain, yet back
to the limit of their range. A single jack had come up
with them and followed their movements, as much
chinook as the biggest of them and as fully mature,
though he weighed less than two pounds. The old man
wondered if the ripe white milt in him would fertilize
the eggs of a female or if an abundance of full-grown
males would keep him and his fellows back from the
redds until they died with their precocious strength
still in them or uselessly spent on the unreceptive

rocks. It was a queer link across the width of a continent that there should be precocious males among both
Atlantic and Pacific salmon, yet it seemed one more
of those infinitely subtle provisions that his mind so
loved to turn over and fit into place. The active, fighting males, gaunt and scarred, well advanced towards
death while the females still seemed strong and perfect,
were a weakness in the plan; the little jacks covered
the weakness; the price of their maturity was the death
of life scarcely half lived through but, used or unused,
they had provided a safety factor, filled a purpose.

The fish settled at last, still uneasily, just below
where the slope of the bottom came up from deep
water to the shallows at the tail of the pool. The Senator stood up, stretched his tall old body and started
reluctantly along the trail towards his house.

It began to rain that night, a heavy rain with half a
gale blowing up from the south, and continued all the
next day. For the first time since June the river began
to rise. Soon it was up several inches and a little
colored. The growing current sought out Spring and
increased her restlessness. She forsook her position
above the brown boulder altogether and worked down
towards the tail of the pool. There, with many others
of her age and kind, she held, facing upstream against
the current. From time to time one or other of them
would stop swimming and let himself be carried back
almost to the lip of the pool, only to find a sudden
drive of fear in the fierce drawing of the current which

started him up into the pool again. Spring was full of a restless, unsatisfied eagerness. Again and again she dropped back, often with a whole group of the others, only to find fear and swim up again.

While the little fish hung there, struggling with their reluctance, awaiting the strength of a final stimulation to brave the broken current of the rapid, spawning fish of the year came past them up into the pool on the rising river. They were great gray shapes which Spring scarcely noticed and more rarely tremendous flashes of which she was hardly more aware. She was filled with her own urgency, her own fear, and the same urgency, the same fear was communicated to her again by the quick uneasy movements of the other small fish near her. The final stimulation came to her and to some fifty other young chinooks in the fading light of a September day. They dropped back and back in an almost compact group, started up once or twice from the draw of the current, finally let themselves be carried over the lip of the pool and down into the rapid, still with their heads upstream, still swimming against the current.

At the time she left the pool Spring was a fraction less than five inches long. The sixteenth concentric ring was just forming on her scales and over her river colors, her spots and parr-marks and the olive green of her back, first traces of silver were beginning to show.

## Chapter Seven

WITH her passage over the lip of the pool Spring was in some measure released from the pull of fear and restlessness that had grown in her through the previous week. Among the other small migrants she was drawn down the rapid, swimming against the current composedly and vigorously, yet not strongly enough to hold against it. The whole fifty or sixty of them kept together in a compact and ordered school, each holding position and distance from the others. At first their formation was roughly diamond-shaped and they were carried down rapidly in a run of broken, heavy current. They worked gradually across this and finally swung in behind the shelter of a big rock near the right bank, where they held easily for a considerable time. Then, still moving together, they let themselves be drawn on in the downstream journey, riding securely in the broken water, individuals among them occasionally taking insects that passed within easy reach.

Little more than half an hour after leaving the pool at the foot of the canyon they reached the next pool downstream. The quarter-mile drift through the rapid seemed to have taught them a new assurance, for they turned at once on reaching the comparatively still water and swam directly downstream with the slow current. But at the tail of the pool they hesitated again, swimming in quick uneasy circles where the current began to draw strongly over the shallows. A few individuals let themselves slide on down at last and the rest followed, tail first again, swimming so strongly that the four- or five-knot current carried them down less than a mile an hour. They came to the pool at the wide bend near Senator Evans' house, swam through it and let themselves down into the next rapid. Their passing was silent, invisible, without trace, though the lighted windows of the house looked down upon them as they passed. This traffic of the river could only be hidden and unheeded, having in it the nearness and the infinity of distance that the passing of men in a crowded street has, or the passing of cars on the night highway. Before sunrise the little school of fish had broken its journey in a pool six miles farther down the stream.

With the growth of daylight much of the restlessness and exhilaration of the seaward movement drew away from Spring. It was still near her, all through the new surroundings of the strange pool, in the autumn-freshened water that touched her, in the movement of the other fish of the school; but it no longer possessed her and for the time being she was content to hold in the easy current and feed upon whatever came to her. She knew a pleasure in the strength and activity and sureness of her body, still not fully confident and strong, having in it the furtive swiftness and the sudden sharp movements of the creature that many other creatures seek to destroy, but growing always more positive and more positively felt. She moved forward to intercept a mayfly nymph rising to the surface, her body taut so that the muscles showed long lines under her silvering scales. A moment later she swam swiftly to the surface of the water and broke through it in a leap that carried her a foot into the dry air. A strong surplus of energy was building up in her and in the others of the school. In the fading light of that day they left the sheltered water and went on down the river.

But the three-hundred-mile way they had to follow to the sea was not the clear, clean way of their ancestors. There were poisons in it and obstructions across it and false ways leading from it. On the third night of their migration Spring and the school with her entered a long reach of slow water. They followed it down, threading a way among drowned tree stumps under the right bank; near the tail of the reach they felt a smooth draw of swifter current and turned at once to head into it. It was an easy current and they were content to be drawn down with it; it grew stronger, but smoothly and gently, and they showed little sign of nervousness when they reached the moving screen across the intake of the power canal. The beat of their small bodies increased a little so that they held themselves from being carried against the wire mesh; in perfect unison the whole school swung across the face of the screen, searching a way down. Once or twice they swam up a little way, then let themselves be carried down again. Little by little they worked farther out into the stream. The draw of current was suddenly fiercer; Spring and some of the others fought against it and won across to a gentler flow. The rest of the school passed down with it into the comparatively easy passage through the broken steps of the salmon ladder.

Perhaps a dozen fish held on with Spring across the fore-bay of the dam. They found easy water a little way below the surface, but they were not content with it and came up again into the draw of the spillways. The gliding strength of this water and the thundering vibration of its fall terrified them, yet drew them also. They fought it, made way against it, fell back. They went down again, came up again. The glide of the swift water above the easy water was stimulating in its terror and Spring jumped twice, clear of the water, heading upstream. Around her other small fish jumped and the school broke up into individuals. Spring relaxed in the water, letting herself be carried by it. Almost in the smooth curved lip of the spillway she began to fight fiercely again, winning briefly against the tremendous flow of the water. But she knew a need of fast water which held her near the surface, swimming strongly until at last she tired a little and was carried out over the lip of the spillway, tumbling in the steep fall of white water to be tossed upward again where it broke at the base of the dam. Briefly she was lost in a light, a brittle world of bubbles and foam, jolted and battered in a thunder of white water, helpless, almost drowned, terrified. She came out of it, gasping and unbalanced, into a dark eddy behind a sheltering buttress of the dam.

Other migrating chinooks were resting in the eddy and a new school, larger than the one she had lost, formed itself around Spring from the scatterings of several schools. For a little while the big school milled and circled in the eddy, then the strong purpose, strongly felt in blood and muscle, forced the fish back into the broken water. Spring turned with the others, heading upstream into the rush of the tailrace, and was carried on down.

Below the dam the river was smaller, robbed of nearly half its flow by the canal, but there was still plenty of water for the passage of the young fish. They traveled very little by day, perhaps because the daylight travelers had been reduced almost to extinction by their enemies in the shallow water of runs and rapids through thousands of generations of migrating chinooks. Each evening, shortly after sunset but before full darkness, the restlessness drew the school on again and the young fish journeyed down some eight or ten miles before the light of the next day grew strong. They spent the daylight in the shelter of pools or the larger eddies, feeding upon what they could find easily. About them the valley widened gradually, drawing away from the timbered hills. The stream's hurried tumbling pace slowed a little, but it carried on, clear and rippling, through flowing pools and broad bright rapids, until its valley met the finest farm valley of Oregon. There it slid easily into a greater stream, joining without fuss or spectacle, creasing the surface for a few yards, then lost in the breadth of the smooth quiet flow.

Spring was little conscious of the change. The water was less clear, there was a bottom of clay or small gravel much of the time in place of the big round boulders of her native stream, rapids were few and easy. But she had used only a small part of the pool in which she spent her first year and now she was conscious only of that small circle of the larger river immediately about her. The school found sheltered water easily at each daylight pause of its journey, often in a bay eaten into the soft bank or on the inside of a long slow curve, and turned only a little more hesitantly back to the main current at each dusk. Food was scarcer than it had been before and at times they traveled with little or nothing in their bellies, though they took without hesitation whatever came near them.

The new river, though immediately bordered by alder and willow, cottonwoods and maples, flowed through broad low farmlands that rolled away to hills and mountains already distant. The farmhouses were well built and well cared for, the barns fat and full; in agriculture the valley had not altogether forgotten its capacity for nourishing fine trees—stands of fir and oak, neatly ranged as plantations and sharply cut from the fields, flourishing maples and locusts, fine groves of walnuts and filberts, orchards of prune and cherry trees and down from these to long rows of berry bushes, all were given soil on equal terms with vetch and clover and grain. And, that the good of the soil might be released to their use, from time to time part of the river's flow was diverted.

A few days after reaching this new river, towards dark, the school began to move restlessly about a sheltered eddy in which it had spent that day's light. The fish had turned down as usual, and a little outwards, seeking the draw of the current. They felt it, sliding unnaturally across the lower end of the eddy, and swam up from it uncertainly. A few fish broke away and worked directly out across the eddy, into the main current of the river; in a brief moment they had passed from reach or sight of the others. The main body of the school circled in the eddy for a short while longer, then went down into the current that cut across the lower end. The current took the little fish quietly to itself, drawing them with a smooth, deceptive flow that slid easily along shovel-scarred banks of earth, away from the river and out into the fat farmland. After their first uneasiness they went with it gladly, letting it carry them when it would, turning to swim with it when the flow was not strong enough to please them. In their own knowledge they never became lost because the guiding current was with them almost to the end, drawing them or leading them constantly towards what should have been the sea. But in reality their migration had long since become a vain wandering through mile upon mile of wide carriers and narrow ditches. Late in a dry October they became cut off in a stagnant pool at the bottom of a drying ditch. They died there at last, flapping and struggling in the liquid mud. They were few, a tiny migrant band that had found a blind end to its journey. But in the spring and early summer other thousands found the same false way and the same unnoticed death in the fertile farmlands of the valley.

Spring traveled on with the reduced school. There were not more than two dozen of them now, but they kept well together in the easy flow of the stream. The current was seldom fast enough to keep them near shore and for the most part they held well towards the center of the stream, taking advantage of the best flow, but they still headed up and swam against it except in the very slowest reaches, so that they seldom dropped down more than ten miles in a night of traveling. Their journeying was composed and somehow dignified by calm unhurried purpose. There was strangely little in it of haste or exuberance yet they were filled, all of them, with a splendor of strength and energy that sometimes revealed itself. They played one evening in the gentle run at the head of a pool where they had rested through the day. The red sunset light was on the water, rolled in soft, darker lines by the flow; a hatch of flies was drifting down. The little fish spread along the run, dimpling the surface with their rises, leaping out into the red and gold of the warm October evening, swimming up, dropping back, moving all ways, suddenly released from the solemn purpose that held their traveling. But as soon as the light had left the water they collected again into their school and became once more devoted migrants; they seemed again frail and tiny and humble, lost in the big river, guarded by nothing more solid than chance, the law of averages that might let some of them survive to reach salt water.

They came that night into a wide reach of slow smooth water, more nearly lake than river. They swam down, among drowned stumps and rotting brush again, with scarcely a trace of current to help them. It was a changed way, though they did not know it; a way that had once led their ancestors down to the lip of a tall fall whose broken white had forced them to their grandest leaping in the upstream return to the spawning bed. Carrying, as it was carrying now, the weight of the fall rains, the river still poured over the rock face of the old fall, but it was a changed face, lengthened and rounded by concrete into a long, upstream, horseshoe loop. Spring and her school drew down to it, heading upstream as they felt the increasing pull of the surface water. This time they found the salmon ladder in the center of the dam and passed easily down its concrete steps, resting when they wanted, delighting in the broken bubbling water that gave them oxygen more freely than any they had known in the past several days.

The broken race below the ladder carried them swiftly in spite of their resistance. Soon they were passing tall buildings whose throbbing hum and many lighted windows they dimly felt and saw; there might have been terror in such things, so suddenly found, but if there was the little fish did not show it; they passed, intent as pilgrims, heads upstream and swimming steadily.

So they reached the bad water. The bed of the river became coated with gray slime. The water, no longer bright, flowed evilly over it, sucking behind piles and protruding slime-coated sticks in little whirlpools, hiding its shallowness in gray opaqueness, deepening its depths into foul and poison-filled darkness. The river was flowing at a good level and had the freshening of the early fall rains, but even so the migrants could no longer find in it the oxygen they needed. Spring, swimming near the surface, began to draw water through her gills more and more rapidly. Around her the others were doing the same. Keeping together in the school they swung back and forth across the river as the current carried them down. They were confused and uncertain, near panic, but they sought for better water in this only way they knew, and they did not find it. A few began to break the surface, as though trying to snatch oxygen from the air. Once the whole school dived sharply down, only to come back to the surface again a moment later. Spring jumped right out and fell back, keeping her place in the school. Ahead of her a fish turned on its side, righted itself and kept swimming. Soon after that the current carried them beyond the worst of the pollution. The water became gradually clearer as the suspended waste sank down to foul the bottom. Spring felt her mouth and gills clean again, but the opening and closing of her gill covers was still rapid, almost a gasping movement. It slowed gradually as the current turned and rolled and mixed the water, breaking it against rocks, tumbling it in wavelets, exposing it to the air and restoring its oxygen.

The school rested and fed in good water the next day —water as good, that is, as any they had known for a week, because there had been some pollution in the river for fully fifty miles above the big dam. But now their journey led through heavily settled country and as they went down in the stream each night they passed brightly lighted buildings that clattered with activity— activity that made cream into butter, logs into paper or lumber, hides into leather, wool into cloth and always spewed its waste into the accommodating ditch that had once been a river; the towns added their sewage and for mile after mile the river was never able to rid itself of one pollution before the next poured into it. In all this length the migrants found no other food than a few midge larvae. They were often gasping for oxygen and one or two were carried away from the school, belly up, quite still for yards, then struggling spasmodically to right themselves and hold in the current, then still again with gaping gill covers. Only the force and cleanness of the rains behind the rising river carried the others through. It fought for them constantly, dissipating and oxidizing the effluents, reducing concentrations that would have killed every fish exposed to them for more than an hour or two, providing a meager surplus of oxygen for breathing, washing sediment from mouths and gills, healing and soothing injured membranes.

When they came to the great city through which their river flowed to its union with the Columbia the migrants were still rapt in their struggle to survive. For the first time they passed through water that throbbed with the movement of great ships; there was activity all about them, the bustling of small boats, the heavy thudding of pile drivers, the rattle and squeak of derricks, the flowing of a thousand streams of used liquid to thicken the turgid water. These things were nothing to Spring. She lived in her empty belly, in the discomfort of her hot and swollen gills, in the inescapable drive of her migration. It took all her strength to hold herself steady, staring dully upstream, with fins and body working sluggishly as the current carried her down. It was nothing to her that they spent a whole night's traveling in a reach where lights shone down on the water from both sides, nothing to her that great bridges slipped past far above her; even the great shapes of scavenging fish in the water near her could not move her to flight, and the dip of a boatman's oar, from which she would have darted like a quick shaft of light a week earlier, almost touched her and left her caught in a swirl of water that threw her off balance and gave her a brief gasp or two of better water.

So the slow deep river, lapping at the piles, sucking behind the piers of its bridges, bearing its ships and all the filth of human waste, carried them into the first unfelt influence of the tides. Overburdened with death and decay there was still in it enough of life to support their brief passage.

# PART TWO

## WITHIN THE TIDES

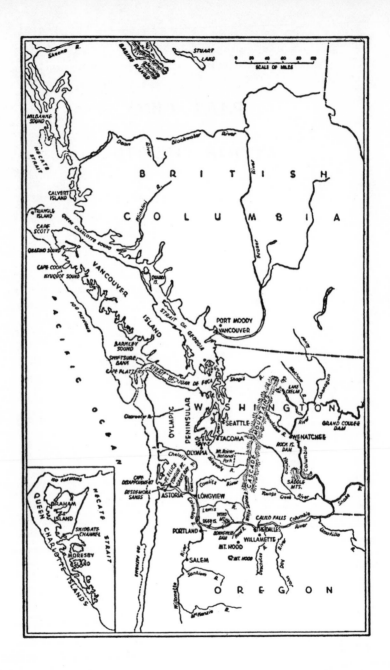

# Chapter Eight

A NIGHT's journey below the heart of the city and still nearly two hundred miles from the ocean the polluted river joined the heavy, mile-wide flood of the Columbia. Gathering the waters of the steep mountain rivers to itself, bearing them on in its still and stately way through the farmlands of the wide valley, passing beneath its bridges and among its wharves in the city, the polluted river had seemed big. Now it was instantly dwarfed, almost instantly lost; its entry, split by a great island, lost something in the division; but even had it been single a man could not have seen that all its depth and breadth and flow added a fraction to the greatness of the Columbia. The Columbia's might grows from the heart of a continent, swelled by the entry of a hundred such lesser river systems; where it accepted Spring and the stream that carried her it is in the full tide of its magnificence, almost complete, one of the great rivers of the world.

At first the change meant little to Spring. She held to her place in the school, moving sluggishly, staring upstream with dull eyes. It was nearly a month since she had left the pool at the foot of the canyon and in that time she had grown less than a quarter of an inch. Her belly was empty now and her gills still seemed clogged and hot; much of her fine energy was spent and she had barely won through a journey that had been glad and easy for her ancestors, a joyous prelude to the fullness and strength of the sea. But as the polluted water lost itself in the breadth and depth of the Columbia she found strength again and a cleanness all about her as the poisons were dissipated in the huge volume of good water. There was food to be had also, a fair plenty of it, though still far from the generous abundance of the Canyon Pool in August. She began to breath easily through soothed gills. All about her was the stir of other migrants, in large schools and small schools—fish from Washington and Oregon, from Idaho and British Columbia, fish from above Bonneville, above Rock Island, above Grand Coulee, for that great dam had not yet barred their way; fish from the Willamette, the Deschutes, the Yakima, the Wenatchee and a hundred other spawning streams; above all fish from the Snake, best-loved of all spawning waters by the spring-running chinooks, fish from its great tributary the Salmon and perhaps even a few, very few, from the murdered run of the Clearwater.

The broad and solemn gray-brown of the river, sweeping past wharves and piling, swelling over the sandbars in deep silent folds or shallow murmuring ripples, was little marked by the passing of the migrants. They let themselves down easily in the strong current, individuals among them jumping occasionally but the great majority intent upon their journey. From time to time the whole river throbbed and beat with the passing, upstream or down, of some ocean-going ship. Nearly always there were boats of one sort or another near them, rowboats or power boats, fishing boats drifting, pulling net, plugging back to the cannery or to a new set, tugs fussing over great rafts of logs or surging squatly towards new assignments. It was a busy river, highway to a great city and the productive states behind it. The tiny traffic of the little fish descending, even that of the great fish of the late fall run that passed them on the upstream journey to the spawning grounds, made little mark.

Yet once the passage of the chinooks had made a mark that no one could miss, even in that wide, full-flowing river. The Douglas firs stood tall and straight on the hills above the river then, all the way from the mouth of the Willamette to Cape Disappointment. The cities were not cities then, the Hume canneries were not built, there were no irrigation ditches to trap downstream migrants, no haphazardly constructed dams to shut off thousands of acres of spawning grounds from ascending fish, no factories to foul the water with their wastes. And the splashings of Spring's ancestors whitened the broad river from shore to shore. The chinooks leapt in the pride of their strength and passed on up in great schools, near the surface, thrusting arrowhead ripples ahead of them. Steelhead leapt there freely and the little Columbia bluebacks, passing through in their thousands, tightly schooled and near the surface, showed the river a patchwork of moving figures of color to the early woodsman who paused to look down from some high bluff. The silvers and humpbacks and dog salmon milled and played off the mouths of the lower tributaries and the sturgeon passed unseen then as now, well down in the deep channels. But each spring and fall without fail the river was live and broken with the boldness of the great chinooks. That they are not so much to be seen now may be in some measure because those with the bold leaping blood showed themselves too freely to the fishermen and because the great ships and all the stir of the river make the rest shy and cautious. More certainly, more directly and more simply it is because there are not so many of them—not one-fourth, perhaps not one-tenth of the numbers that ran just seventy years ago, when the timber stood.

In the night they reached the Columbia, Spring and her school traveled some three or four miles down the river before daylight turned them to rest and feed in the shelter of a sandbar. They were still sluggish and almost feeble, but they had worked over from the left bank towards the center of the river and were in good water, recovering rapidly. Spring searched the gray water about her and found chironomids rising through it occasionally. Behind a barely submerged hump in the sandbar which sheltered the school there was a rippled line of rejoining currents, and along this surface insects collected; the little fish rose to them quietly, touching the surface with tiny dimples that were almost instantly lost. But there was no real plenty of food even yet and the school slipped out and found the current again well before dusk.

In the big river they traveled a little faster than they had before, quite often in daylight, because they were safer in its great breadth and depth and because the silt-bearing water hid them from too strong a light and the searching eyes of their enemies. But enemies passed over them from time to time—eagles and ospreys, cormorants and, more and more frequently, the ravenous, searching herring gulls—forcing them to turn quickly down to deeper water. In the depths there were bullheads, many times larger than those in the Canyon Pool, wide-jawed and hungry. They passed among these dangers without the protection of fear, because fear would have delayed their journey, halted their feeding, broken the necessary order of their lives. But they were helped and driven by quick fear and quick reaction as soon as any danger became immediate.

They passed under Longview Bridge in the night, tasting pollution again below it. It was noon, two days later, somewhere off the mouth of Abernathy Creek, that they came in the path of the *Pacific Shipper*. The *Shipper* was bound upstream, to take on apples at Portland for the British Isles. Spring was aware of her as a great looming shadow in the midst of a thunderous vibration that had passed without harming her many times before. The shadow was new and terrifying and she sought to go down, away from it. The hissing bow wave caught her with the rest of the school and tossed her out in a tumble of foam. She struggled, found her balance and drove herself down through the water. She saw the squawfish clearly, open-mouthed and very close, swung from it and went up again; behind her it turned down, the struggles of a slower member of the school satisfyingly in its gullet.

A raven swept on slow black wings across the river, two or three feet above the surface. The shadow of his passing met Spring as she came up from the squawfish. She turned from it less wildly; the raven dipped, hovered, went on. A pale wide-winged shadow drew swiftly to his movement, drove a curved yellow beak below the surface. A moment later the gull was riding smoothly in the still disturbed wake of the *Shipper*, a second fish from the school gleaming silver in his beak. He threw his head back and swallowed. Spring and the rest of the school were already many yards downstream, deep under the surface, beyond sight, beyond fear. They continued downstream, heading into the current, until an eddy behind a small island drew them to feed.

Danger did not often crowd them so closely. Many gulls saw the school as it was passing over deep water, hesitated briefly on braking wings, then passed on. As the shadow crossed them the little fish sank a few feet deeper, slowly and deliberately, without changing the speed of their journey, then rose again as slowly. When a big fish drove at them from below they darted up, scattered and panicky, jumping clear of the water, turning and twisting, sending the encouraging flashes through the water behind them; usually it was the end of the migration for one or more of the school. But the school was not constant. Other schools joined it, traveled with it briefly or for long stretches, broke away, leaving room for yet others to join. At all times there were a hundred or more migrants in the water about Spring, traveling at the same pace, turning as she turned, resting as she rested, belonging with her. Sometimes there were as many as a thousand. The toll taken by the predators, birds and fish, was steady and large; but it left no mark upon the survivors.

Two or three days after the upstream passing of the *Pacific Shipper* the school came suddenly upon the gleaming, twisting bodies of half a dozen great chinooks. The bodies were invisibly restrained and suspended, but a line of dark floating blobs at the surface dipped and sent out ripples as they struggled. Two fish grew still and hung with spread gill-plates as Spring passed under them; she felt the touch of the net's twine along her side and swam quickly up from it, frightened. The current took her down again and she passed easily through the mesh, whose width was nearly twice her length. Above her the cork-line moved and the shining bodies of the chinooks moved with it. Later the school passed through other nets which held struggling fish; the flashes of the great bodies held no warning for Spring and she had felt terror only at the chance touch of the twine of that first net.

As they worked down the river, past the low-lying islands with their small farms and splendid cottonwood trees, past the orange-buff gashes that stood out against the dark green timber wherever the road cut through a point, past the sandbars and past the drift-lined beaches, the influence of the tide began to make itself felt. Off Cathalamet, where Puget Island broadly splits the river and the mountains mount steeply from the south shore, the tide mark shows clearly, several feet of dark silt-gray dampness on the piles at low water. There was still no faintest trace of salt in the water, but from this point on the migration of the school became less constant. A chart of its course would have seemed confused and almost purposeless, marked by delays in slack water or turned back upon itself by contrary currents; but the sum total was always downstream, towards the plenty of the ocean, until they came to Desdemona Sands and turned among the piles under the canneries of Astoria.

Here they found food in plenty, suddenly and easily. The fish-packing boats were still bringing in late-fall chinooks and dog salmon, from gill-netters and drag seiners, from traps and trollers; the machinery roared in the canneries, the gang knives clanked and rattled, cutting the fish for the cans. The offal poured down into the water around the piles, hearts and livers that were called waste and the great swollen ovaries with their thousands upon thousands of smooth, shining, orange-scarlet eggs. The migrant schools turned in from every direction towards the feast and hung on the downstream side of each cannery until the water was black with them. For nearly a month Spring held there and fed in the midst of a threshing, driving, competitive multitude of migrants. Above them the gulls screamed and struggled, breaking up the larger pieces of offal. Below them Dolly Vardens, squawfish and bullheads grew too fat and too lazy to prey on bright living things that could move away.

Spring grew fast. On her scales the concentric rings began to widen and record this intermediate growth, more rapid than that she had made in her own river or during her migration but still much slower than that she would make in the sea. Her whole body was now overlaid with silver, veiling parr-marks and spots until they were invisible except from certain angles and in certain lights. Like all animals whose safety or food depends in any degree upon concealment, she was dark on the back and lighter below; her back was a strong steel blue with fresh black spots in it; her sides were silver gray shading to pure silver and then to clear white on her belly. Her tail was spotted and forked and the fineness of the wrist above it was emphasized by the increasing bulk of her body.

By the end of November she was more than six inches long; a full inch of her growth had been made during the month she had spent under the cannery and, though there were individuals among the migrants still larger, she was at least half an inch above the average size of those collected under the cannery. Throughout the whole busy, active month her belly had been full, yet she had never lacked the drive and strength to compete vigorously for food whenever it appeared; had the supply of offal continued her migration might have been delayed through many months, but early in December the cannery closed and the flow of easy forage was over. Spring hung hopefully nearby for two or three days, picking up such trifles as the current brought to her. But her belly was no longer full and there was a new restlessness among the young fish about her. Schools broke away from the main body and disappeared. There was constant stirring and circling and searching through the water among the piles. Then Spring found herself in the middle of a school of about two hundred fish, working away, out and down river; the piles became dim shadows standing faintly in the gray water; very soon they faded into the wall of grayness that edged the circle of Spring's vision.

Astoria is a little more than half way down the wide estuary of the Columbia. More than twenty miles long, nearly ten miles wide from Grays Bay to the Oregon shore, the estuary would be a great gulf opening upon the Pacific Ocean were it not for the weight of fresh water pressing through it and forcing the ocean to keep its place and halt its salt tides to the west of the line between Astoria and Point Ellice. In a man's ordinary conception a river can have but little part in filling and sweeping such a place; the winds fleet across it and drive spume from the wave-tops; from the Oregon side the sawmills and canneries of Washington are slim plumes of white smoke against the heavy green mountainsides; from the Washington side Astoria is flattened into a dwarf and hazy city; Astoria itself looks down river upon an infinity of water that is still for a long time the Columbia before it becomes the Pacific Ocean.

In all the scope of the last ten miles of this great estuary Spring found yet more delay in her journey. With the school that had left the cannery she crossed the strong deep flow of the ship channel between Astoria and Desdemona Sands. The tide was ebbing and for the first time there was a taste of salt in the water which made her feel buoyant and strong; she swam with quickly moving tail and body, heading up into the current but drifting down with it as she had all through the long migration. Angling easily across, feeding upon what was swept down to it, the school was carried seawards by the current for nearly a mile before it reached the slacker water along the sands.

Here Spring fed easily, ranging over the shoals in the eddies of the returning tide. She found reddish copepods, queer-shaped, small, swimming with active strokes of feathered oarlike arms, and took them eagerly; occasionally a chironomid or some other winged insect was carried down on the water and crossed her sight; more rarely still she flashed in quick pursuit of

Asellus the sow-bug, so like a wood-louse that one might easily have supposed he had slipped into the water from some floating chunk of rotten wood, or the jerkily swimming sand-hoppers whose sideways-flattened bodies drew across her vision in always curving passage.

The school fed out the flood tide on the sands, ranging, driving and pursuing for the first time as they would through their whole saltwater life. But there was still a restlessness in them and on the start of the ebb they swung out once more into the current of the ship channel. A strong wind from the Washington side raised short broken waves and piled the flow in towards the deep bay below Astoria. The young fish were carried gradually across in the drift and as the flood tide started to make they found themselves within the eddy of the bay. There was food there and they fed, working gradually deeper and deeper into the sheltered water, away from the flow that would have carried them on out to sea.

## CHAPTER NINE

IN YOUNG'S BAY, just below Astoria and within ten or twelve miles of the open Pacific, the school became trapped for several months. They were not trapped in the sense that they wished to get out and could not; but within the bay their immediate desires were satisfied; they found food in plenty and the shifting tides made a confusion of currents that carried them back and forth, this way and that through a maze of journeying that satisfied any urge towards downstream migration that may still have been in them. The strong winds of winter added to the confusion, driving currents before them, stirring the short-crested waves, drifting food to the shelter of the bay so that it became a minor ocean within the river, an adequate training ground for the dangers and necessities of deep water.

Spring learned to feed in the active searching way of salmon in the ocean. The school was constantly moving, following the drift or the positive movement of what it preyed upon. Northerly winds from the Washington shore drove the plankton deep into the bay and drew the fish after it. More frequent southerly winds led them out again towards the channel, but the prevailing set of the eddying current held much feed against this drift and from the heart of the bay towards the shelter of the Oregon shoreline there was always a concentration of both drifted and free-moving food. Spring and the school she was with fed close to shore through most of the winter, often finding the adult copepods in vulnerable masses that made easy foraging. Day after day the school followed the flood tide up over the beaches, picking up the brown and pink and blue-gray sand-hoppers easily as the returning water stirred them from feeding on piles of weed that winter storms had broken away and left stranded.

By the end of January, Spring was nearly eight inches long. The parr-marks and spots, all her freshwater coloring, was completely hidden by a veil of silver crystals. Her scales were growing steadily as the evenly spaced, wider rings of intermediate growth built up around the freshwater nucleus. The other migrants of the still-changing school were nearly always within an inch of the same length and so exactly like her in marking and development that only the missing adipose and ventral fins marked her apart from them.

Feeding or resting, the migrant schools held well together, usually within a few feet of the surface of the water. In the Canyon Pool, Spring had always sunk down among the rocks on the bottom to rest. Now, whenever her belly was full and the strong urge to feed had briefly left her, she rested with the school in mid-water, cushioned and drifting in the gentle subsurface swell from the violent winter storms. Over them, in the quick and scattering waves, there were nearly always ducks—goldeneyes, mergansers, butterballs, mallard, teal, bluebills, harlequins and many others, driven in by the greater storms outside. High above these there were birds of prey at most times of the daylight; occasionally gray-blue darting peregrines that chased the strongest flocks to the water just for the sport of it, because their fierce, quick brains and pulsing muscles craved instant satisfaction of the urge that sight of movement stimulated in them; Cooper's hawks, less wanton in their lesser strength, but sure and deadly when a weak or crippled bird came within reach; the bald eagles, ponderously efficient in finding cripples, always ready to battle for the kill of a swifter, more successful hunter; and the ospreys, strong keen hunters of fish, whose prowess served the eagles best of all.

The ospreys ranged widely over the estuary, searching for slow-moving coarse fish but plunging down upon young salmon whenever the schools offered themselves too near the surface. The bright clear days were best for them and a spell of frosty weather in February set them working keenly over the rippled blue surface of the bay. Almost in the breaking of the brittle waves there were copepod larvae, drawn up by the sunlight. Spring fed upon them with her school, cruising easily along close under the surface. An osprey slid down from the Oregon shore, riding into the strengthening northwest breeze. He soared on it, for love of the day and his living, graceful and harmless five hundred feet above the water. He set his wings and slid away half the height, soared briefly and slid away again to within fifty feet of the water. Then he began to hunt in earnest, working over the bay on long smooth strokes of his big wings. His neat white head, with a crest of dark feathers and the sharp, curved beak, turned this way and that as he flew. His pale eyes, small-pupiled in the bright light, saw movement of many things in the water below him. He changed his flight suddenly, hovering, rising a little in the wind, then his straightly upstretched wings and long downward-straining legs converted his body from plane into plummet and he drove down. He hit the water and disappeared into the splash. A moment later he was in the air again, flying on slow wings a few feet above the water. A few yards from his dive he checked his flight briefly and with a strong tremor of wings and body shook the water from his feathers.

He rose again to a fair height above the water, still heading into the wind; he moved ahead slowly, swinging back and forth in searching. He saw the school of feeding migrants, side-slipped directly over it, hovered briefly and made his dive. Spring had seen the shadow of the osprey's coming and had darted away from it. All around her she saw the flashes of the flight of the other migrants. Behind her, under the shattered surface of the waves, she saw the long legs and pale-gray reaching talons. Fully two feet under water the bird's strong claws gripped into the back of a nine-inch chinook. The small fish struggled, but the rough underside of the osprey's feet and the curve of the claws held him firmly. The osprey beat his wings and rose from the water.

The wind had freshened strongly and he tried to rise into it, but the added surface of the flat side of the fish slowed him down. He shook the water from his wings, struggled a little farther, then dropped back to the reaching waves. He lay there for a few moments, resting on outspread wings, his head raised and his fierce eyes looking about him in every direction. He rose again more easily and made headway into the wind. His grip on the fish was changed so that he now held it along the line of his body, its head towards the wind.

He had risen to a good height before he saw the eagle. He slid away instantly, downwind and towards the shore. But the eagle was an old bird, wise in his method of hunting. His fine head and broad tail shone brilliantly white in the sunlight and his broad black wings were carrying him swiftly to intercept the osprey before the sliding turn was fully made. The eagle came up to him and drove down. The osprey dipped, tumbled away, recovered. He was down within fifty feet of the water, but the eagle came at him again. The osprey dropped his fish and half turned in the air to defend himself. The eagle was past him with a rush of wings, intent upon the fish as it shone silver in the sunlight. He caught it easily above the water and swung upward. The osprey went back to his ranging search of the bay and in a little while stooped again, killed again and kept his prey.

Spring lost little time from feeding through her fright. Danger passed and repassed many times in every day; she turned from it in swift reaction and forgot it as soon as it was beyond the reach of her senses. There was a measure of safety for her in the number of small fish always near her, to intercept the stoop or dash of preda- tors and send them away temporarily satisfied. She was not wise or cautious, but her muscles were quick in re- sponse and amply strong to turn or drive her small body swiftly towards safety. She was of a good design for the life she lived and guarded and nothing, not even the Senator's mark which showed in scar tissue where the fins had been clipped away, impaired her performance.

The cold bright weather held over the bay through February, but in March there were southerly gales which blew for days at a time and piled the water away from the Oregon shore towards the main river channel. The current which returned to the main flow of the river at the upstream end of the bay was accentuated, and the general set of currents all through the comparatively slack water, except close under the Oregon shore, was outwards. By this time Spring was becoming a really sizeable fish, ten inches long or more, and her ever-increasing appetite sent her ranging more and more widely in search of food. As the winds held, the ranging schools of young chinooks all through the bay were gradually drawn after the drift of the feed in the new currents; they followed it out, feeding, and turned along the line where the easy flow from the bay met the strong flood of the river, still feeding. All along this line of the two currents the drifting feed collected, sometimes caught in pockets that eddied back into the bay for a little way, sometimes carried on to go down and out to sea with the river, but for the most part held and moving only slowly in the very edge of the river's flow.

Spring and her school fed across the line and out into the strong current, then cut back, slashing across it again into the bay. On the flood tides the eddies that cut into the bay, against the wind-driven currents, were strong and wide and held the feed well. The little fish used them to the utmost. Under the gray waves, on the face of them, on the backs of them, sometimes even in their crashing crests Spring cruised smoothly and calmly wherever the copepods or sand-hoppers or other creatures seemed thickest. On the ebb tides the eddies smoothed out and turned back towards the river current, carrying fish and feed with them. So, quite slowly, with many slants and deflections in their journey, Spring and her school were carried out and down towards the great bar at the mouth of the Columbia.

Several times when it seemed that they were securely caught in the heavy flow of ebb and river, the strong rush of the returning flood flung them back upstream again. They crossed the bar and finally reached the open sea on an early morning late in March. There was no wind to break the surface of the water, but the great swells of a dead storm rolled in from the open Pacific, piling steeply against the current swells of the Columbia's heavy mass of water. A pale-gold sun came up over the Cascades, lost in hazy mist, and its cold light was gold and white and gray on the silent hills and hollows of rolling water. A tug wallowed up from the south jetty with a raft of logs. Spring and her school passed near it and found in their passage land creatures, wood-lice, termites, even one or two grubs and beetles that had dropped away from the logs. Across the middle of the bar, with tide and current at her back, a tall freighter, light-loaded, followed the migrants down. She seemed to shake her head in the swells as she smelt the full salt of the open sea ahead of her.

## Return to the River

Spring was buoyed in the water. She felt strong and eager as she rolled her dorsal fin out into the gold light on the face of a great smooth swell. She rode up with it, the rest of the school close around her in the water, and on the crest leapt into the air; her silver scales flashed their own brightness back into the pale sun and she leapt again while the eyes of the lookout man on the freighter's bow were still on the splash of her first break. The freighter drew up to them and the little fish turned down and away from its approach. Before the tide had turned they were well out among sandbars over which the Columbia's huge flow spread to lose itself in the ocean.

Spring had fed her way out across the bar and she fed on through the rest of that day and for many days after, turning with the school wherever the forage seemed thickest. Though it was still early in the spring there was a richness of feeding greater than any she had known. Near the surface, often in masses, were tiny creatures in tremendous quantity and variety; larvae of barnacles and copepods, crabs and shrimps and a host of other sea creatures, produced in their myriads to build the bodies of vigorous hunting creatures such as Spring, and still leave survivors to breed a new abundance.

After leaving the river the school had been drawn almost quickly across the strong flow that pushed out into the ocean, towards the more sheltered water behind Cape Disappointment. Here, above the piled gray mud and sand brought down from Oregon, Washington, Idaho, Montana, British Columbia in thousands of years of the river's flow, they found eddying currents and strong rips where the feed waited for them. Once again they were trapped, as they had been in Young's Bay. Nothing barred their way or held them in; they had more than the strength to drive them through the strongest of the eddying currents. But their incentive to movement was all within the few square miles where the cushioned tides turned back from the core of the Columbia's flow. Only a greater hunger or the positive passage of some prey drawing them after it could free them to follow their journey to its limits.

## CHAPTER TEN

FOR some weeks after reaching the open sea Spring fed near shore, in fairly shallow water. She began to pick up larger food than the copepods and other small larvae that came to her so easily, and the strong satisfaction of swift pursuit, the seizing of solid, heavy prey and the pressure of her distended belly afterwards led her to keener hunting and wider ranging. The school began to work gradually away from shore, still among the rips and eddies of the Columbia's slackening flow, but in water steadily clearing itself of suspended mud and sand and always growing deeper. Four miles offshore, over nearly a hundred feet of water, they came for the first time upon the pink feed.

Spring saw ahead of her, and above her in the water, a mass of moving creatures. Around the edge of each translucent body there was a halo of orange-pink light that stirred something inside her; she turned up with the school and drove at the mass, seizing the crisp, inch-long bodies in her jaws, turning them, swallowing them as fast as she could. She fed until the mass was broken and lost, fed among the flashing bodies of her fellow chinooks, of herrings almost as large as they were and of bulky savage fish that came from below to feed upon the feeders. She fed without fear, without caution, without pause until her belly was full and she was heavy and slow and temporarily satisfied. The school cruised lazily, feeding little for several hours afterwards. For the pink feed, the Euphausid shrimps, *Euphausia pacifica*, call it what you will, is one of the most generous abundances of the Pacific Ocean, and it is the salmon's own food; chinook or blueback or silver, chum or pink, they are all directly or indirectly dependent upon it in all their saltwater years.

But it was still early in the year for real abundance of the pink feed and it was some while before the school again found them massed. Meanwhile they ranged and searched through the water, traveling westward and always a little northward as the river current fanned out. The water under them became twenty fathoms deep, then thirty fathoms, then fifty. And they learned to go down in it, searching through the dark depths during the daylight hours when much of the feed went down, following it up towards the surface again as the light drew away.

Spring grew and thrived. Constant feeding deepened her body and built muscle solid and wide across her back. Each day she became more the hunter, less the hunted. There were great creatures all through the water about her and she was still small, scarcely larger than a full-grown herring; but she was becoming a pursuer, a predator in the fullest sense of the word, and the intensity of pursuit in fierce competition with the other young chinooks in the school was the constant controlling factor of her life.

Not many days after the school had found the massed Euphausids Spring moved a step further towards adult feeding habits. She was swimming easily along the edge of a tidal eddy at the time, some eight or ten fathoms below the surface. There was only a dim light at that depth and the other fish in the school were faint shadows around her as they foraged. Tiny creatures revealed themselves by ephemeral flashes of phosphorescence in the heavy blueness; she responded automatically, almost lazily, turning this way and that to take them as they showed. Then a broader flash than these pinpoints struck suddenly back at her from less than a foot away; she felt the nearest of her shadowy companions converging sharply towards it and drove herself forward; the flash struck back at her again, nearer, turning; she turned as sharply and her jaws closed for the first time on the satisfying, resistant bulk of scales and firm flesh.

Carried on by the speed of her pursuit, but with tail and body still, she held the smelt in her jaws; then she turned it and swallowed it as though she had never known any other way of feeding.

In the summer months the Euphausids became really numerous and Spring fed upon little else. She found them massed near the surface at times, but they were all through the water, often in dark depths where their tiny phosphorescent lanterns, each with its lens and reflector, revealed them. At this time the school was ranging in water about ten miles offshore and usually between forty and fifty fathoms deep. But the bottom was uneven, with ridges and hills and banks of rock or shale or hard clay standing up from the general level of gray sand and mud. Behind each rise the strong tides built an eddy which collected the drifting plankton, visible and invisible, and this drew the larger animals to mill and feed until the tide changed and dispersed the drift. Within these eddies life passed through many stages, the same stages and in the same way as it had in the Canyon Pool. The smallest creatures were the first to collect as an eddy formed—diatoms in tremendous numbers and variety, Asterionella, Thalassiosira, Navicula, Coscinodiscus and very many others, some of them differing scarcely at all from those in the Canyon Pool. These were passive and still, the first link in the chain, converting the sunlight, absorbing minerals from the water into their bodies. Among them were the tiny suspended eggs of many marine creatures, drifting without will and without protection. And then the rotifers and flagellates, feeding with quick and busy movements but still at the mercy of the currents, and with them the larvae of barnacles, mussels, snails, sea slugs and even oysters.

A little above these, feeding upon the diatoms, there were the copepods, Calanoids and Harpacticids, and after them the Euphausids and the squids. Then the stage was set for the fish. The herrings came, all sizes of them shining silver in quick movement, and sometimes the launce fish, close packed in their schooled thousands, heads to the current, slender bodies rippling with the swimming movement of eels. The light of their bodies as they fed drew other fish, large and small, preyed upon and preying. Big salmon slashed through schools of herring and needlefish, filling their bellies, making the growth that would bring them to quick maturity and the return to the rivers. Small chinooks like Spring were there, and the bluebacks, feeding chiefly on the Euphausids, cod of all kinds and all sizes taking Euphausids, herrings, launce fish and young salmon; near bottom great bullheads and often halibut weighing a hundred pounds or more.

Amid this fierce competition and its sudden dangers Spring spent the whole of her second summer. She was cushioned and held, turned and drifted and guided by the ocean; she moved after food, turned for it, went up or went down in search of it, but the ocean moved the food and often enough carried her too without the least effort on her own part. By September she was some way north of the mouth of the Columbia, still along the fifty-fathom line and well out from shore. She was with a school of fifty or a hundred fish, all about her own size, a fair number of them fish that had wintered with her in Young's Bay and perhaps five or six fish that had left the Canyon Pool with her. Of them all she was the only one that bore a mark.

The school came at this time into a wide and deep eddy that had formed behind a long bank of gravel which rose sharply to within twenty-five or thirty fathoms of the surface. The feeding was good in the eddy and Spring gorged happily on Euphausids and a plenty of young squid. These were the slender arrow-like opalescent squids, most of them between one and two inches long and just starting to make the rapid growth that would bring them to their full ten inches in six or seven months' time. They moved about their feeding swiftly and easily, turning this way and that to clasp small creatures in their tentacles and carry them to their mouths. Spring pursued and caught them with her own swiftness, exulting in the movement, in the pressure of water against her and the flow of it along her sides. She chased a squid almost into the open jaws of a forty-pound cultus cod, turned away at the last moment and intercepted another squid. She saw the shadowy form of a great skate, fully six feet long, and kept away from it, still feeding. Then suddenly she felt fear; it was all around her in the water, in the swift fleeting of herrings, in the quick flight of her own school, in the urgent driving of her own tail and body. She went down and away into black depths. Two great blue sharks, slender, graceful, swift and always hungry, came down into the eddy. They cut through the water silently and easily, gliding rather than swimming, turning a little to catch and swallow the slow cod and rockfish. They hunted and found and fed without pause, quartering back and forth through the eddy like giant bats hunting flies and moths in the dark evening air. When they had passed on their way the big ray came slowly up from his hiding on pectoral fins that waved in silent motion with something of the breadth of elephant's ears. From another direction the cultus cod returned. They saw each other, faintly luminous in the dark of the deep water; the cod's gloomy eyes seemed to signal his resignation to a persecution that could not be resisted. The ray turned lazily and the eye-like spot on each pectoral showed briefly in the dim light.

Spring lay without moving on the face of the bank for perhaps thirty minutes after the sharks had passed. The school lay round her, silver bellies pressed to the gravel, dark backs motionless and invisible in the darkness. A lamprey slithered its eel body across the gravel, stopped, slithered on and came to rest near one of the young chinooks. Very slowly it raised its sucking mouth and ugly head. Still slowly and gently it set the sucking disc against the side of the fish, just above the anal fin. The disc gripped and the young chinook stirred slightly. For several minutes everything was still in the darkness, then the lamprey's teeth began to rasp at the silver scales and the young salmon stirred again. The teeth bit through into the flesh and the salmon started sharply up from the bottom, carrying the lamprey with him. He circled uneasily and then, as the teeth rasped deeper, drove upwards in an agonized attempt to shake the pain from him. He came down again with the lamprey still holding and once more was motionless on the bottom as though he could lose his enemy by hiding. One or two fish in the school had stirred slightly as he struggled and gradually the whole school came to life. For a little while they hung on scarcely moving fins just above the gravel, then they moved off to search for food again.

They found it quickly and easily a little way along the bank. It was well up in the water behind a high point on the bank and the small bright flashes of herring among larger flashes of feeding adult chinooks drew them to it. The Euphausids were there and the school turned immediately to feeding. The big late-fall chinooks were feeding lazily, mature almost past desire for food but stirred in spite of themselves by the easy prey. A hundred feet above them a small boat passed slowly across the surface, riding the long easy swells with her sixty-foot poles spread to carry trolling lines. A fifty-pound ball of lead passed behind Spring, almost touching her tail and sending her upwards in panic. A slow, wobbling, injured creature sent the halting flashes of its distress back to her and she turned from that too as a big chinook passed her and struck fiercely at it. The chinook gripped the injured thing, held it and a moment later was himself jerked fiercely into flashing struggle. In the dark water the light of even his great body was visible only briefly, then drawn beyond sight.

That evening the school rose close to the surface in pursuit of the dusk migration of copepods and the other feeding creatures that followed them. The young fish carrying the lamprey was still with the school, but he followed erratically and with difficulty. Several times he left them to swim to the surface at his best speed, jump out and fall back. Each effort left him weaker and the lamprey still clung to him, gnawing at the living flesh.

A full moon lighted the herrings as they fed on the copepods and drew cod and dogfish upon them. The weakening chinook circled his own school as they fed, but fed not at all himself. Even there, five fathoms down, his erratic movements caught the moonlight. A big cod drove at him. Another, still larger, came from below to intercept his flight. The wide jaws gripped his silver body firmly and carried it off into the darkness with the lamprey still trailing.

Summer passed into the fall that started Spring's third year. Fall became winter and there was less feed on the banks. Spring and the school ranged widely, searching and gradually working northwards through the great open ocean storms. Spring had spent a good first ocean year; she was about sixteen inches long and weighed well over two pounds. Between thirty and forty new concentric rings, widely and evenly spaced, had built up on her scales; even with the coming of winter they showed little sign of narrowing and only the sharp increase of growth at the start of the next summer's feeding would show her age clearly.

## CHAPTER ELEVEN

THAT first winter of ocean feeding carried Spring far beyond all influence of the Columbia River. The southwest gales blowing up towards Cape Flattery strengthened the set of the northward tides and aided the drift of feed and fish. The school found good feeding off Destruction Island and worked out as far as the halibut banks more than twenty miles offshore, where the continental shelf begins to drop sharply down towards the twelve-thousand-foot soundings of the real Pacific. Through most of the winter the young salmon were fairly deep in the water, but in late February and March great numbers of adult copepods moved up near the surface to breed. These had been feeding between fifty and a hundred fathoms down since December, in their brief adult stage. Now they had ceased feeding; their mouths were no longer able to grasp or chew the diatoms and other small things upon which they had fed through a year of life. They had only to breed and then die, empty-bodied and with all the delicate parts of them broken and disordered. The fertile eggs of the females would join the mosaic ocean drift to hatch out and develop through six larval stages and five later stages to a similar maturity and fulfillment.

The ascent of the copepods was followed by many of the larger creatures that fed upon them; and Spring followed these. She was in light water again, riding the great swells, rolling her back above the surface at times or jumping clear out into the spray-filled air. She found Euphausids often enough in fair plenty, though not the plenty of summer; often she hunted the little short Rossia squids and occasionally she caught a small herring, a sand launce or one of the true shrimps. Loligo, the slender arrowlike squid she had caught for herself in the previous summer, was there also; swift and graceful with a lovely iridescence in the light water, they were too large for her now—perhaps they were also too perfectly designed, for she had no movement, no quickness of turning or speed of flight, that they could not match.

In feeding and drifting the northward movement of the school held to bring them past Cape Flattery and up to Swiftsure Bank early in the June of Spring's third year. On the bank the migration paused. Here, where the Strait of Juan de Fuca ran out like a tremendous river between the Olympic Peninsula and Vancouver Island, was a crossroads of the salmon's world, where all the Pacific species passed and repassed; the north- and south-bound Columbia chinooks met the homing sockeyes of the Fraser River and all the complicated traffic of pink salmon and silver salmon passing between the Gulf of Georgia and the open sea. The hundred-fathom line swung far from shore, built out in glacial silt and valley mud, in sand ground from rock by wind and river and sea through the hundreds of thousands of years that the rivers had flowed into Puget Sound and the Gulf. Among the submerged hills and valleys of the bank the currents swirled and twisted, met together and came back upon themselves in such ways that the drift of the seasons eternally collected there and was held to attract and satisfy free-swimming creatures.

As she came to Swiftsure Bank, Spring measured nearly twenty inches from the tip of her nose to the fork of her tail and weighed a little less than four pounds. She had been feeding well for two or three months past, turning more and more to pursuit of the bright herrings and pilchards and launce fish, whose silvery turnings struck back through her eyes to her brain and stimulated the increasing vigor and strength of her muscles to drive and strike. She was already learning to look for the strong sensation that flowed into her from the struggle of a firm, scaled body securely gripped across the middle, and the calmer yet equally strong satisfaction of a belly packed and heavy with fish. But on Swiftsure Bank there were Euphausids again, Euphausids in thousands upon thousands so massed that she could dart in, take several at a mouthful, gulp them and open her jaws to take more while the others were still in her gullet. There was strong competition on Swiftsure Bank. Many chinooks of all sizes were there; the young silvers in their first sea year cut into the massed Euphausids, and their elders, maturing, drove launce fish and herrings to the waiting sea birds at the surface in a fury of eager feeding that their rapid growth maintained almost constantly. Early in July the maturing sockeyes gathered from their mysterious ocean ways, gorging themselves on the Euphausids for a last time before hunger left them; in a little while they had to find the Fraser's current in the Straits and follow their fasting journey to its conclusion above the lakes in the heart of British Columbia.

Feeding as they fed, Spring was often near the sockeyes. They were slender fish, a little finer-scaled than she was, quick and graceful, with the silver sides and bluish backs of deep-water feeders. They were efficient gatherers of crustaceans—Euphausids, copepods and even smaller creatures with which Spring no longer concerned herself; they had fed in the same way throughout life and their many-toothed gill arches, straining the water that passed through as they breathed, made them better designed than other Pacific salmon for such feeding.

But the sockeyes were a prize. The canneries waited for them, sure of a market for their firm red flesh in the cans. In the Gulf and in the Fraser itself the gill-netters waited. Off Sooke in the Strait of Juan de

Fuca the traps waited. And the big deepsea purse-seine boats went out to meet them on Swiftsure Bank. There had been trollers out there all through the summer, and Spring had seen their wares many times, wobbling with slow, compelling movement through the hazy water. Once or twice, when they passed close to her and her whole attention was not held by some real fish or feed, she turned after them; but each time another chinook or a silver was ahead of her and she saw its struggling body jerked on and away at the same slow speed of the wobbling spoon bait.

The first of the hungry purse-seine boats came out to the bank at the end of June. She ranged widely, searching for fish, her skipper at the outside wheel on the flying bridge above the pilot house, watching the gently moving water for bubbles or ripples, anything that would show him where to make a set. He set twice and caught only silvers. A third set, nearly twenty-four hours later, rounded up a small school of sockeyes. Boats that had been catching only silvers and chinooks began to get sockeyes. Other boats came out to the bank. By the end of July they were getting sockeyes, chinooks, pinks and silvers in about equal numbers, but they searched always for sockeyes; watching for bubbles, for fish on the pink feed, turning away from the finning chinooks and the silvers that jumped out and fell back on their tails or drove the launce fish out of the water in rainbow showers ahead of their savage feeding. And in this there was danger for Spring who was still feeding as the sock-eyes fed, often with them.

Several times boats passed near her and there were nets in the water within a few hundred feet of her. Young chinooks and silvers were caught in the sets and thrown back dead or dying, crushed by the weight of fish in the purse of the net or injured in the brail-ing. But it was not until the middle of August, when the fishing was at its greatest intensity, that she was circled by a cork line. It was a still day, clear and sunny, and she was feeding with the school only a few fathoms below the surface. A large school of sockeyes was feeding with them on the same concentration of drift.

The seine boat passed near and her captain saw the bubbles from the feeding fish. He swung the boat over sharply. In a moment the skiff-man was over the stern and in the big skiff towing behind the boat; someone cut the skiff free and the skiff-man was rowing strongly to anchor the end of the net while the crew paid out cork line, lead line and web from the turntable on the stern of the boat. The boat began her circle, the cork line bobbing in her wake, the lead line sinking fast and the web sighing and bubbling as it touched the water and was drawn down.

Spring felt the vibration of the heavy diesel engine and the big wheel through the water. It built her nerv-ousness, already strong from the brightness of the day and the shallow feeding place. The set was slightly misjudged and cut across the school of sockeyes, enclosing little more than half of them. The lead line, passing among them and drawing the web down after it, disturbed them and drove them from their feeding. Spring saw and felt their hurried flight; it was too much for her and with the other chinooks she sounded, swimming straight down for deep water. Above her the set was complete. The boat had returned to the skiff. The cork line made a full circle and the crew was hauling the purse line over the niggerheads to close the bottom of the net and trap the fish that were already making the corks bob up and down on the smooth water. Spring held to her flight, straight down. She struck the rising web suddenly, near the purse line, turned away from it, then sharply down again, seeking the bottom in full terror. The purse line drew the web on over her and left her free, but a dozen young chinooks were trapped and drawn up with it. The net came in and the circle of corks grew smaller and smaller. The fish milled and swam uneasily as it narrowed. They became terrified, tried to plunge through the web. But they were drawn steadily in to the side of the boat until they were milling and flopping and struggling without room to swim. The giant dip-net lowered from the mast and brailing began. Net after full net was lifted and dumped aboard. The water foamed white alongside the boat; tails showed in it, dorsal fins and clean silver sides. It was a good set.

As August drew on into September more and more

salmon passed over the bank. The last of the sockeyes passed through almost hurriedly, not pausing to feed. The pinks poured through in greater and greater numbers, filling the holds of the purse seiners. Fall chinooks passed southward in the journey to the Columbia; the silvers came faster and faster until the middle of the month, stirring the whole bank with their vigor. And then, almost suddenly, it was over. The purse seiners caught a few silvers in the early part of October, then pulled out to look for dog salmon elsewhere. Only the trollers held on to the tag end of October, catching a few silvers and fewer chinooks for their pains in facing the strengthening storms. Already spawned-out fish were dying in the rivers. The great annual migration was past and Swiftsure Bank was left once more to feeding, immature fish.

Spring fed there. She was two feet long, a salmon-sized salmon. A flash of movement in the water meant food to her now, not danger. She drove into schools of herring and needlefish, scattering them and seizing them in the security of her strength. As long as she found food easily she was content to stay on the bank, but with the coming of winter food became harder to find. The pilchards had turned southwards to California on their spawning migration long before. The herrings were turning towards sheltered water in the Straits, in the Gulf and in the great Inlets, in a movement that would bring them to their spawning in lagoons and shallow bays that following February and

March. The chinooks and silvers had to search and range for their food again and Spring's slowing growth showed in the narrowing scale rings of her third winter.

The gentle tides of the banks were never constant. In each twelve hours, day and night, they swung clockwise through all the points of the compass; over them was a steady non-tidal current, setting northwestward except where the steady westerly winds of summer turned it back upon itself. In the fall and winter winds from the south the current became strong in its true direction, bearing the drift northward and westward across the mouth of the Strait and along the Vancouver Island shore. Searching through the water Spring was caught up in the current, enclosed in it, carried with it. At times she turned into it or sheltered from it in feeding behind some bar or bank; but in sum it continued her migration, carrying her always northwestward along the shore-line, away from the mouth of her river. By the spring of her fourth year she was off the mouth of Barkley Sound, well up along the coast of Vancouver Island. She was coming into the long stretch of water that the big American and Canadian trolling boats work steadily from March until September of every year.

# Chapter Twelve

Senator Evans had fished slowly up from his house to the tail of the Canyon Pool, covering the heavy runs and deep glides with his bushy Oregon deer-hair flies. The broad creel strap pressed on his shoulder and he moved slowly into position to start covering the pool. A little unwillingly he admitted to himself that he was almost tired—not really tired, but he could remember when the stretch from the house to the canyon had seemed too short for a day's fishing. Now he was just going to give a few chances to the big red-sided rainbow that always rose out in midstream at the head of the shallows, then go up on the bank to sit quietly for a while before starting home.

He noticed one of Gunner's fyke nets set at the edge of the current in the lower end of the eddy. Don was starting to collect food samples, to get a check on the productivity of the stream. With luck he might be along that way during the afternoon. The old man turned back to the pool, making a few false casts to lengthen his line and dry the fly. It was early in May and the water was high, too high really for good fishing and tolerably easy wading, but he had had good fishing that day; the six fish in his creel were all well above his self-imposed fourteen-inch limit and there had been few of the eight- and nine-inch "tourist" fish to drown his fly. The big fellow would nicely cap the basket, if he came.

He made a cast, shooting the heavy fly line coiled in his hand; the fly landed prettily a yard above the usual holt of the big fish and floated down ahead of the up-stream curve of the gut. Nothing moved to it and he cast again, floating the gray-hackled fly along the same line. He made half a dozen more casts, searching water inches to the left of his first cast, in towards his own bank. There was no rise, but he had not expected one. If the fish were away from his usual holt he would be slightly farther out, in deeper water and stronger cur-rent. He set the fly again on the line of its first drift, then six inches farther over, then a foot. For a big fish in smooth water the rainbow rose sharply, rolling his red side out and over. The old man tightened on him, felt his first run up the pool, checked it and brought him back. There was no jumping, but the fish ran again for deep water. He was hard to check and hard to lift, but the old man sensed a sluggishness in his fight. He freed his net, lifted hard and brought the fish back to him easily in the current. The red side showed broadly and the twenty-inch length looked too long as it slid over the net. The belly was dark and sunken on the flanks; the jaw was long and the square tail seemed over-large. The old man held the ring of the net above water and looked down at the fish still floating in the mesh. Don Gunner asked from the bank: "Not good enough?"

The Senator looked up smiling and shook his head. "We'll expect better things of him in the fall. He's nothing better than a tired old rake just now."

He bent down and freed the hook easily, holding the shank firmly between thumb and forefinger and pressing away from the buried point and barb. The exhausted fish lay on his side almost without movement. The Senator lifted him out of the net and held him in the water, head upstream, until he found strength to swim slowly away.

Gunner waded out, lifted his fyke net and carried it back to the bank.

"No more fish?" Gunner asked.

"No more fishing," the old man said. "I've been promising myself that big fellow to top off the basket all the way up here. But I've got enough anyway."

He set his rod down, unstrapped his creel, then settled himself on the ground with his back against the base of a stump. It felt good to be there, off his feet and resting, with the warmth coming into his legs through the wet waders. The water was cold in the spring for old blood. The sunlight through the fresh pale alder leaves was good and he watched it quietly for several minutes before he reached for his pipe.

Gunner came up from his net and sat beside him.

"Good catch?" the old man asked.

"Just the usual. Plenty of mayflies and caddis and stoneflies. I'll have to start getting quantitative samples soon now; this business doesn't tell you much, but it teaches you what to expect and makes identification easier when you come to the main job—if they let me go on to it."

"Why not? What's the trouble now?"

"Hatcheries again. They're putting in racks to catch up the whole run of chinooks."

The old man sat up straight. "The hell you say." He felt shocked and almost physically sick as he realized the full implication of what Gunner had said. No salmon passing up the river, no salmon ever again spawning in the Canyon Pool. New days and new ways; many things had been destroyed or driven out of Oregon in his lifetime, and an old mind could not always see the good of what came in their places. But this was hardest of all to take.

Gunner went on: "Of course, they'll put the fry back in the stream pretty soon after hatching, I guess— they'll have to unless they build acres of rearing ponds. So it may not affect what I'm doing now. They'll have to find food just as though they were hatched naturally."

"Where are they going to put in this weir?" the old man asked.

"They've got it in already, just above the first highway bridge."

"Then they really will get the whole run—it's not more than five or six miles from there to the main river. What sort of a rig is it?"

"Just a simple rack. You've seen them—tripods made

of poles and weighted with rocks, and slats nailed on."

The old man nodded. "I guess that puts an end to our little experiment," he said.

"Which one?"

"The marking. It'll be three years this summer since I marked that first lot with the left ventral and the adipose. They'd be back year after next—or perhaps even next year."

"I was thinking of that the other day," Gunner said. "They're following right along with their tagging program up in British Columbia—I had a letter from Charlie Wilson and he's out on it again this summer."

"Charlie Wilson," the old man searched his memory. "I ought to know who he is."

"He did that paper on chinook movements off the west coast of Vancouver Island. He's good. I worked with him at Cornell."

The old man nodded, frowning at himself. "Sure, I know now. He's a bright boy. Takes more chances than some of you biologists."

"Well, he'll be watching for our marks. And they may pick up some of his tags down at the rack."

"Yes," the old man said. "Down at the rack, but not up here in the Pool. You know, Don, I'd like to go down there with a hammer and knock some of the slats out of that rack when the time comes."

Nearly six hundred miles from the Canyon Pool by the route she had followed, Spring fed on the salmon banks of Ucluelet. She was three and a half years old and weighed between six and seven pounds. By the beginning of May the warmer water and stronger sunlight were already producing something of the midsummer abundance; the diatoms were multiplying and the phosphorescent dinoflagellates showed in patches of red water by day and living light by night. Globigerina lived among the other plankton, grew its hard shell of limestone, multiplied itself and died to sink down through thousands of feet of water and add its hard shell to the myriad millions of others that made the gray ooze of the deep ocean floor. The pace of it all quickened steadily, summoning copepods and Euphausids, true shrimps and jellyfish, crab larvae and the wing-footed molluscs; the herrings were there again in great schools, sand launce and squids came up from deeper water, pilchards nearing the end of their northward migration from California, anchovies, flat fish, all swam and fed and pursued their being in the light water. Dogfish and sharks, skates, rays, big cod and salmon, porpoises and seals and even whales were on the banks. Spring took her place in all this, one step farther removed from the original source of life in the sunlight that multiplied the diatoms. She fed almost constantly upon the herrings and sand launce and pilchards; in their bellies were copepods and in these were diatoms whose hard shells endured the triple attack of digestion and, as the pressure of her constant feeding forced them on, fell away from Spring to sink to the bottom.

Over the feeding fish the deepsea trollers worked, their tall poles spread like out-riggers. They were efficient units, far removed from the Indian or earlier white man towing a home-made spoon or a herring on a hook behind a dugout canoe near shore. They were diesel-powered, thirty-five, forty, even forty-five feet long, thoroughly seaworthy. Their main poles were sixty feet long, each dragging two stainless-steel lines which carried several spoons apiece and, when the fish were deep, as much as fifty pounds of lead in a single round ball. Lines from the stern and from bow poles made up a total of twenty or more spoons to send their slow, halting flashes through the water and draw the chinooks and silvers from pursuit of safer prey. And they fished steadily when the fish were in, from dawn till dark and often for days on end, carrying ice in their holds so that they could stay at sea without fear the catch would spoil.

In three or four seasons of tagging off the Island Charlie Wilson had learned to love the West Coast trolling fleet. It seemed to him that the fleet and its boats and its men were a perfect symbol of individual effort. He stood now in the stern cockpit of the *Kathleen*, watching the other boats of the fleet as they gradually showed up in the light of a sun not yet over the horizon. It was a calm morning, with great swells rolling in from mid-Pacific and the boat riding them like a seagull, with roll so slow that it seemed no roll at all. Red was up forward, making coffee, and the smell of it came back to him there in the stern. He rolled a cigarette and lit it. The fish were late about taking—that pre-dawn light was often the best of the day, but in a few minutes now the sun would be up. He wondered what the other boats were doing and tried to see through the faint light; but it didn't matter much. Red was always on the fish as soon as the others were. He pulled hard at the cigarette; the morning mattered, and being there, out on the banks, with big spring salmon somewhere below and the red sun rising over Vancouver Island.

He thought back to the trollers again. They gambled money, real money, in their deepsea boats, gambled it on their own skill and knowledge against the vagaries of fish and weather and prices. He thought of their good little co-operatives, of their generosity towards newcomers to the fleet, of their easy willingness to help one another find fish or tide over a period of bad luck; and then again of their independence—a cursed independence, often enough, but fitting, in key with the job, somehow matching the great hog-backed swells that came out of nowhere, lifted the fleet as though it were a scattered group of coracles and rolled on for twenty miles more to crash white on the gray rock shores of the Island. He looked forward at Red and smiled as he thought of the big man's contempt for the small-boat trollers of the inside waters. "They haven't got enough guts to get away from their farms and make a dollar. A man can't make salt fussing around in the Gulf like that and they know it. But they stay there and beef." Red had taken a twenty-foot open gasboat to fish off Narwhitti Bar when he was a kid of eighteen. Out of that season had come a bigger boat and out of the good and bad seasons that followed had grown the *Kathleen*, with her thirty-five diesel horsepower.

Happy Hammond's boat passed close, Happy smiling in the stern as the bells on his poles danced and sounded from the vibration of his old engine, and signaling "No fish." Happy had overloaded his boat last year and lost it with everything he possessed aboard. Lucky Johns had picked him up and here was Happy back on the grounds again, still happy and quiet, a little apologetic, talking over his tongue as though unwilling to let the words out when he did talk, but always catching fish when there were fish to be caught. Lucky Johns was out again too, one of the few boats not using steel lines. Lucky had gone overboard a few years back; his linen stern lines were fishing shallow and he had grabbed one, then reached across for the other and pulled himself back to the moving boat, hand over hand on the two of them. Lucky couldn't swim, so he stayed with the linen lines.

A bell jingled sharply on the outside line of the starboard pole. Charlie reached for it and threw in the clutch on the gurdey. Red stuck his head out of the pilot house. "Hell," he said. "We would have to start pulling fish just when I get breakfast ready."

The gurdey, powered off the engine, reeled in the line. Red held a thirty-pound chinook while Charlie set a numbered metal tag at the base of the tail and expertly picked away a few scales from below the dorsal fin with a light forceps. Red put the fish overboard. "One," he said. "Use your notebook and pencil in a hurry, boy. We'll be moving from now on." The bells jingled on both poles and a fish hung on one of the stern lines.

## CHAPTER THIRTEEN

LIGHT comes before sunrise, coldly, intensely reflected from an eastern sky deepened away to vast distance. There is a sudden shiver in the time that shakes away the things of night before the coming day. On the West Coast salmon banks at those times was a great stirring of creatures; different forms of plankton were moving vertically up towards the light or down away from it as their needs directed them. The plankton feeders followed and big active predators, salmon and cod, the sharks and the night-feeding dogfish, kept close after them. Much of the movement was towards deep water, but in the pre-dawn both fish and feed were, for the most part, still near the surface.

The salmon especially were always well up in the water at this time, nearer the surface and more active than at any time through the day until dusk. All generations of salmon before Spring had moved to feed by the early light, matching the activity of other creatures stirring to the change. Even when there was little else near them to move or when, on their spawning migration, the desire to feed had left them, the salmon still moved, for the change of light itself touched them directly.

Spring had responded to this stimulation of sunless daylight all through her life in salt water. It fostered an actual physical effect within her body, a chain of physical releases and changes that impelled her to activity. In much the same way a shift of current or a suddenly increased flow thrilled her body into activity and searching. On the morning that Charlie Wilson found time to watch the trolling fleet as the rising sun lit the grounds Spring had responded, as usual, to the earliest trace of light. The school of chinooks had been resting on the northward face of the bank along which most of the trolling boats were working, and almost as the fish began to search they found a concentration of squid in the water above them. Spring fed on the squid for nearly two hours, following their movement, driving down through them, resting briefly in deep water below them, turning up again, gliding away again. As the light grew she seemed a greenish shadow, long and strong, with a liquid, silent quickness in the water. The other fish moved about her in the half-lighted depths, gliding, feeding, turning, resting in their own ways and at their own times so that they

formed an intricate pattern of silent, effective movement. As they fed a local set of tide came on to the
sheltered northward face of the bank, carrying the
drift towards the forming eddy on the southward face.

Spring did not notice the change except as the freshening flow stimulated her to a greater fury of activity.
She was lost in the gliding, silent movement of herself
and her companions, part of a smooth dance that went
on and on as long as the squids controlled it. Little by
little in the changing water they became split and scattered and the feeding was less easy and the rhythm of
movement became subtly broken. The herrings were
already collected in the eddy to southward of the bank
and Spring turned upon them as their hazy silver
flashed in the green water. She struck at them once,
carrying a herring away in her jaws for several yards
before she turned it and swallowed it. Many salmon
of many sizes were feeding and above them in the early
sun bells jingled sharply at the tips of trolling poles,
the strong springs jerked at the head of the lines and
the gurdeys ground fish up towards the boats. A halting silver flash, hazy as those of the herring, struck
through the water to Spring's eye and drew her forward in a rush that was matched by another fish of
the same school. Spring reached the limping thing,
struck at it, held on and was brought up in a jarring
shock. The second fish turned down in a long curve
and struck at another spoon. The weight of his strike

jarred Spring again and she fought. Both fish fought, twisting their bodies, striving downwards against the steady upward draw of the line.

The *Kathleen* rode easily along the bank, little waves of a gentle westerly lapping at her sides on the face of the broad swells. Red Gifkin was back in the cockpit; both men had managed to eat and drink hastily between fish and Charlie Wilson had rolled and lighted another cigarette. Red noticed the double strike on the outside starboard line and set the gurdey to work.

Wilson said: "It's a good day. You'd better hang on to the big ones from now on, Red, and we'll just tag young fish."

The line came in and Spring came with it, still struggling but weaker now from the change of pressure and from being drawn through the water by the steady, relentless pull of the gurdey. Red leaned over the side of the boat, lifted her into the cockpit and freed the big hook. She lay on a wet sack, Wilson's gloved hand holding her down as he worked over her, setting the metal tag at the base of her tail fin, taking the few scales from below her dorsal fin. Red lifted in the second fish and Wilson pointed to the scar tissue that marked Spring's missing fins.

"We've got a prize here, Red. Marked fish—adipose and left ventral."

"The hell. What does that mean?"

Wilson was working on the second fish. "Slip her

back in. This one's ready too. She was probably marked in some hatchery—chances are it was on the Columbia somewhere. The only way to find out is to check her age and then see who had that combination when she was released."

Spring felt the cold of the water about her body and the relief of it in her gills. She swam away, not fast, but somehow sulkily, going down. The second fish was released and followed her. The tag showed briefly through the plankton-filled water after the shape of the fish was hidden. The two men looked back over the stern of the boat as though they still hoped to see something.

"Well," Red said, "wouldn't that jar you? Here we are marking fish out in the middle of the ocean and someone's got ahead of us."

"It'll be a mighty long time before we do that again," Wilson said. "I wish I thought that fish would be picked up in the river."

"She went off, all right. Got on even keel right away."

A fish struck and a bell jingled. Red went on talking as he worked.

"Why can't a guy get mornings like this more often? The way it's going now we'll have a thousand pounds aboard by night, besides the ones you keep throwing back."

Wilson watched the line as it came in. "I think you'd make it better if you kept a good log. Marked down all the fish you caught, what the average size was, where you got them and so on."

The fish was large. Red gaffed it, killed it and threw it into the cockpit. Another bell jingled. "Hell," he said. "I can remember when I caught fish and where it was and go back there next year, if that's what you mean."

"No, I mean more than that. You ought to take temperature readings and mark the set of wind and tide, the depth you're fishing and so on."

Red shook his head. "I never was much at figuring things out on paper. I figure it by what I remember from another season and from what Happy or one of the boys tells me. If we don't get fish one place we hike off somewhere else."

Wilson looked up at him and laughed. "Sure," he said. "You'll be hiking for Egg Island and Milbanke Sound as soon as things get quiet here, then you'll come back down to Quatsino or Kyuquot or somewhere."

Red grinned. "That's right. But what the hell: I like the bunch up there—it wouldn't be a season if a guy didn't get up to show them how to pull fish. Lay off me, Charlie. Next thing you'll be telling me I ought to get married and fish the inside waters like the rest of the farmers."

Wilson laughed again. He wanted to go on with the argument to convince Red both for Red's own good and for the strong possibility that his record and other records like it kept by other trollers would add up to important knowledge about salmon. But somehow, for all his excellence as a fisherman, Red was not the type. He had a hard sense and a boldness of action that made the *Kathleen* so often high boat, but those things matched a careless independence of action rather than any cold efficiency. For Red the companionships he desired, the extravagant chances of long runs from one ground to another, a sort of instinctive knowledge combined with mechanical perfection of gear, were enough—more than enough, they were essentials of his life.

"Not that, Red," he said at last. "I wouldn't want to see the *Kathleen* a farmer's boat." He turned to watch the water bubbling up from the slow-moving wheel in the sunlit water. The diesel engine muttered along happily, the shining lines were taut and steady, cutting through the ripples of the surface. A bell jingled, a pole dipped and Red moved to the gurdeys again.

After her release Spring swam slowly down through the water. The desire to feed had left her. She felt two points in her body; sharp sensation in her jaw, where the hook had had its hold, and in her tail where the tag followed her, its brightness alien to the even coloring of underwater life. Between the two points of sensation her body hardly existed and neither stomach nor gills nor muscles urged her to activity. In listless swimming the second fish kept with her; it had been with her, always near her whatever the composition of the school, ever since they had left the Canyon Pool together more than two and a half years before. Now the steady movement of the boat had carried them away from the school, but they clung together in rigid obedience to whatever it was that held them in the larger schools, and so became a school in themselves. They went down past the quick flashes of herring and launce fish, past the broader flashes of feeding salmon and down into dark water. They found the southward face of the bank in fifty fathoms of water and lay there, resting, readjusting themselves.

Some twelve hours later they were feeding again. Spring was slower and missed her strike more often than she had before, but the herring were plentiful and she fed well enough among a school of large chinooks. The big fish turned to chase her when she cut too closely in front of them, but they were too strongly intent upon their feeding to follow the attack at all viciously and both the tagged fish stayed with them for several days. Then, after a flurry of feeding in the dawn light, they found themselves with a school of fish of their own size and life was wholly normal once more.

The summer passed in feeding and the slow northwestward drift. Sometimes they held for many days to feed on the launce fish, which massed not far from the bottom and moved little. Often they delayed for as long or longer in some great eddy behind the sheltering face of a wide bank that split the current and held the drift for herrings and pilchards. Spring was a large fish now, thirty inches long and weighing more than twelve pounds. The pilchards were almost fully grown, nearing the end of their feeding movement and full of the oil and fat that would carry them through their southward spawning journey to California. Spring found them satisfying food and from them she built, in her turn, much of the fat upon which she would draw in her own spawning migration. More rarely she turned back to the crustaceans, the Euphausids and the great-eyed crab larvae, but, though these were satisfying feed at times, only the flashing bodies stirred her to fullest feeding activity.

By September the currents and the chances of her feeding had carried her northwestward a hundred miles from Barkley Sound to Kyuquot. Off Kyuquot and Quatsino and the jut of Cape Cook between them she was closer to shore than she had been for a long while. The hundred-fathom line at the edge of the continental shelf cuts in deeply there, concentrating fish and feed near shore for the trollers. Spring heard the boats above her again, saw the flash of their polished propeller blades, sometimes followed the wobbling spoons as though to strike, but did not strike. In the weakening sunlight of early fall she fed nearer to the surface, even breaking water at dawn or dusk to chase the forage fish up to the waiting sea birds. The trollers reduced their lines and shortened their leads. Seals and sea-lions rested easily on the great rollers that swept in from Japan, waiting upon digestion before they rolled over to dive and hunt again.

Spring and the school of young chinooks found a concentration of small herrings less than five fathoms under the surface in one day's dawn. They drove into them, circling them, turning them up until they tumbled in shining spray on the smooth backs of the rollers. A fisherman saw the movement and turned towards it. Both his outside lines hung fish before he reached the feeding school. Spring drove the herrings out almost under the overhang of the bow pole, then turned down from the sudden shadow of the boat. The herrings were still about her, bright and scattered, and she turned at them again. The breaking light of the spoons came and she followed one of them, side by side with another young chinook. The other fish moved ahead of her and struck, still swimming along the line of the boat. The hook drew into him gently so that he did not struggle but swam on, holding the line slack above the lead. Spring followed him, unafraid. Above them the fisherman swore and reached for his rifle as the great head of a sea-lion showed behind one of the fish on his outside lines. The sea-lion drew his head under and went down. The hooked fish that Spring was following chose the moment to change direction; the pull of the boat on the line tumbled her and she fought it. The sea-lion saw the movement; the shadow of his huge swift body touched Spring and she sounded. The hooked fish struggled in double terror, turning and twisting in checked and frantic flight as the sea-lion seized her. The hook-hold tore away and he carried her up to the surface. The waiting fisherman shot at him and cursed again as he missed. The sea-lion drew his head under briefly, came up again with the fish still in his jaws, shook it and went down again at the splash of a second bullet near him. The trolling boat plugged on, light puffs of steam and smoke blowing away from her exhaust and the copper paint of her bottom showing as she rolled on the crest of a swell.

## CHAPTER FOURTEEN

SPRING lived the winter that started her fifth year in the driving storms of the restless water that lies between Cape Cook and the northern tip of Vancouver Island. The rolling swells came gray-green from the south with surging, monotonous strength that broke hissing white at their crests to pour down, lift again, break again. The wind tore plumes of spray from the breaks, carrying water for hundreds of yards, then hurling it back like buckshot into the heaving sea again. The backs and breasts of the long heavy swells were marbled and patched and seamed with foam and breaking bubbles. The clouds were low, wind-driven also, and sometimes without rain. The wind made rushing sound out of nothing, the wave crests crashed in a slow complicated rhythm and long-drawn hissing that spent itself in running search for shore or rock or ship to break upon. But there was little out in that water; in November an occasional bold purse-seiner, rolling crazily down towards Cape Cook to search for dog salmon, then nothing for day after day and week after week.

Spring rode in the swells and through them. She knew the whip of driven spray on her broad sides as she came clear out in her arching leap and she knew the tumbled turmoil of a breaking crest. She rolled in the troughs, showing nose, dorsal fin, tag and the upper rays of her tail; it was quiet down there while the storm raged from whitecap to whitecap overhead, but there were all the little noises of disturbed water, bubblings and hissings and the soft sighing of unrest before the next lift.

For the first time Spring seemed to belong in a great ocean storm. She had made big growth in her fourth summer, in spite of the short-lived check from the tagging, and weighed nearly twenty pounds. When she rolled her movement had something of the slow weight of the swells; the swirl of her tail near the surface was a strong thing and when she leapt out to crash back on side or belly there was a white break of water momentarily considerable even amid the infinite breaking of a storm. Beside the huge, harmless forty-foot basking sharks, beside the ponderous sea-lions and the sleek mottled hair seals that slept or fished with lazy ease in the greatest swells, she was small; but the strength and vigor of her race and her shining deep-water body gave her a place among things far larger than herself.

Below the surface she was an efficient, adaptable predator, passing easily from feeding upon the small black cod at a hundred fathoms to pursuit of herrings at ten fathoms or less. She was swift in pursuit, a green shadow that forced a way with sureness and strength, and her turning flung a broad flash from her through the thick water. The metal tag still showed in her tail, little less bright than it had been at first; neither she nor the fish that had been tagged with her seemed slower or less efficient than the others in the school.

Though many of the local fish and even some of those from the Columbia turned to follow the herrings into the sheltered waters of Quatsino Sound, Spring's winter feeding held her for the most part well out towards the hundred-fathom line. Along this line the successive whirls of current that carried always north-westward were stronger for the winter winds. She was carried on past Cape Scott, the last point of Vancouver Island, and past the fierce overfalls and tide rips north of the Cape until by March of her fifth year she was somewhere off tiny rock-faced Triangle Island. There were many seals in the water off Triangle Island, more than had been near Spring at any time except during the annual migrations of the fur seals. They lay in the waves, sleeping on their sides, they dived and fished and played, hair seals all of them. Their thick hides were covered by short stiff hairs, fawn mottled with dark brown, but always wet and seeming jet black as their heads peered over the waves or their bodies rolled out in turning to dive.

Usually Spring fed deep down in the water and was in little danger from the seals. The launce fish, which made most of her winter feeding, were nearly always near bottom and showed little inclination to work upward when the chinooks attacked them. But the chinooks were constantly searching through many depths and often enough there was something to draw them upward. Spring ranged eagerly and searched widely with the school as the ocean life of March began the increase that would make her last full summer of rapid growth in the sea.

Her big body demanded much of her and gave her the power to achieve much. She fed near the crest of a bank one morning, cramming her belly with launce fish while the seas rolled and played fifty fathoms above her. Some chance of tide scattered the launce fish and by mid-afternoon she was well up in the water, turning in on a school of young herring. It was one of the first clear days following the equinox and the sun pierced well down through the water, lighting the herrings until they seemed from a distance a whirl of tiny silver leaves, falling, caught up again, mixed and whirled again. Spring saw nothing but that brightness, and sped through the light water towards it. She drove into the herrings, scattering them, turned down upon them again and caught them with each movement. Around her the other chinooks of the school fed with an equal concentration. The seal came from below, scattering the salmon as they had scattered the herrings. Spring had caught the reflection of his head and back as she turned, a brightness hardly less silver than that of the herrings; she fled away from it, upward at first but already seeking a way to break back and go down. Two or three other fish had turned with her, one of them almost at her side. The seal followed them in liquid motion, turning in the length of his own body as they turned, working always to force them up towards the surface, gaining on them for all their speed of flight. Spring drove her body with an urgency she had seldom used, fearing the light above her, seeking always a way to sound. She broke over at last in a sharp roll and went down in a frantic plunge, the second fish close behind her. In an instant the seal had changed direction and rapid strokes of his powerful flippers drew him horizontally through the water to intercept her plunge. He saw that she was escaping him and turned downward a little; his open jaws passed a foot behind her tail, but in the moment of failure his supple body swung round on itself and trapped the second fish in its terrified upward turn from his attack. He followed its tiring flight almost easily and with accurate persistence. It fought hard for life, turning and twisting in brilliant twice-reflected flashes close under the surface, but the seal was always nearer, always below. He turned upward at last, flippers down, small head straining upward on his long neck, and seized the fish in his fine white teeth. He followed the movement through and broke the surface with a blast of exhausted air from his lungs that sounded across the lonely sea. He shook the big fish, hurled it away from him, caught it again and began to chew on it. As he fed he held himself easily in the water, only his head showing. There had been few salmon lately in the waters he hunted and this was the first he had caught in a month of feeding on cod and flatfish and such smaller things as came his way.

The summer's feeding carried Spring away from Triangle Island, across the open water of Queen Charlotte Sound; the halibut boats passed and repassed along the line she followed, northbound light, southbound loaded. White-hulled, their nested dories brown on the stern and with the red flags of the skate buoys showing above them, they rode the heaviest seas as though they belonged in them. In bad weather leg-of-mutton sails, brown on either side of yellow exhauststacks, steadied the hulls and helped the engines. On calm days the throaty song of their multiple-cylindered diesels sounded across the empty sea with tireless haste that screwed the sea miles out from under their sterns.

By mid-June Spring was up off Milbanke Sound, where Red Gifkin's fancy had taken the *Kathleen* to fish through that part of the season; but she passed well out beyond the banks he worked, gradually drifting and feeding her way across the mouth of Hecate

Strait to the southwest coast of the Queen Charlotte Islands. Two or three times on the journey she passed over narrow channels of deep water where the hundred-fathom line cut far up into the Strait. Off Moresby Island the ocean floor dropped away quickly and Spring was closer to shore than she had been since leaving the influence of the Columbia. Off Graham Island, in the winter of her sixth year, she reached the limit of her range. Through December she fed over a shallow cod-bank, ranging little, held to the bank partly by the good feeding, partly by a new habit of swimming easily against the current when it ran hardest.

Spring had reached her full growth by this time; she was about forty inches long and weighed a little less than thirty-five pounds. There were fish in the school very much larger than she was, some of them weighing fifty pounds or more, and there were many fish considerably smaller; but all or nearly all of them were at the end of their outward journey from the river. They were still feeding, storing fat now rather than making growth, and over the cod-bank they found an abundance of launce fish that fitted their need well.

A great shoal of cultus cod used the bank, moving from side to side of it as the tides shifted. They fed voraciously upon anything that came near them, dog-fish, launce fish, crab, herring or salmon, anything they could catch and compass with their great mouths; they would have fed gladly upon each other except that they were all of about the same size, between twenty-five and thirty pounds, and occasional attempts at cannibalism usually ended in choking death for the attacker with his victim wedged in his throat.

On calm days out-of-season cod fishermen came to the bank, needing fish for food or trap-bait, or to sell to the nearby spruce camps. A boat came out early in the new year and anchored on the bank. The fisherman killed his engine, moved aft and dipped two herrings from a live box. With quick movements he set a large hook in each one, just behind the head, and dropped them overboard on short leaders. The leaders were fastened to one end of a steel rod which also carried several ounces of lead; he dropped rod and lead overboard and paid out heavy cod line until the lead was resting on bottom. Then he settled himself and waited, knowing that he was a little early for the tide.

Spring had seen the shine of the herrings through the water as the lead carried them down. She swam over towards it. The herrings were swimming together in clockwise circles at the end of the leaders, held short of the cod line as they crossed the steel rod, held again as they went out to the limit of their circle at full stretch of rod and leader. Something in their movement held Spring back. She made a quick rush and the herrings broke away from her, then resumed their clockwise circling. Spring's movement drew another fish from the school; he came past her, ran at the herrings, then turned sharply up and away from them. Spring rushed again, seized one of the herrings across the back and ran on with it. The fisherman felt the pull as her rush lifted the lead from the bottom. He let a little line slip through his fingers, then held it. The jerk tore the hook from the herring and left it across Spring's jaws; she went on a little way, then turned it and swallowed it.

The fisherman drew in his line, re-baited, and dropped the new herrings overboard. Twice more Spring robbed his hooks and once another salmon was ahead of her. Then the cod began to come in. They came near bottom, moving slowly, feeding as they moved. A flatfish stirred up from the sand and was caught. A two-foot dogfish, circling near the fisherman's herrings, was seized in the crushing grip of a thirty-pound cod. Spring hung warily above a bottom that seemed covered with fish. The herrings circled still in their clockwise circles and a great cod watched them. He moved forward slowly, took one herring into his wide jaws and lay still. Suddenly his mouth opened again; for a tiny fraction of time the herring seemed held in water between the two great jaws, then it was sucked like a leaf down into the gullet. The fisherman pulled line above, hand over hand, keeping it coming; the cod followed upwards without struggling. The fisherman lifted him over the side of the boat and snapped him off the hook and into the live box in a single movement. He re-baited, threw out his lead. For an hour afterwards he pulled fish steadily.

Within Spring changes were taking place. Up in the front of her body cavity, close above her pectoral fins, eggs were forming in the ovaries. They were drawing shape and form from the flesh and bone of her body, breaking things down to do it, changing things, releasing things. From the first start of the changes had come the stimulation that had caused her to hold, for nearly a month now, resistant to the current drift that had controlled her large movements through the past four and a half years. As the pace of the changes quickened the stimulation grew within her and began more definite response to stimulations outside her. Two days after the cod fisherman had visited the bank a change of tide strengthened the northwestward flow of the current at almost the exact moment of the first pre-dawn light. Spring's blood flowed strongly through her; vibrant muscles drove her up into the current and the rest of the school followed. For perhaps five miles she slid southeastward through the current, feeling it in her mouth, with the thrust of her tail, in the tubed and sensitive line along each side of her body. As the light grew strong and the first flow of the current slackened, the stimulation newly released within her drew back into itself and rested. The school turned down to feed on the launce fish clustered on the sheltered side of a rock ridge that cut out from the coast across the ocean floor. But the journey was started, the change was set.

## PART THREE

## THE FULLNESS OF THE SEA

# CHAPTER FIFTEEN

SPRING reached the limit of her feeding migration more than six hundred miles northwestward of the mouth of the Columbia River, within a hundred miles of Alaska waters. Though she did not begin her southward movement until early January her habits had been gradually changing for several weeks previously. The furious frenzy of feeding and searching for food that had filled her life through nearly four years in the sea had been developing into quieter, more deliberate movement; for hours at a time she lay motionless on the bottom or fed lazily, still near bottom, on the launce fish. The urgency of building and growing was over; she was complete or almost complete within herself. The easy feeding near bottom only served to sustain the bloom of strength at full, that it might stand boldly enough, even while breaking down to seed, to cast the seed where and how it should fall.

The first pause in the southward migration held the school for nearly twenty-four hours. In the shelter of the rock ridge they fed with something of the old vigor and quickness, still driven by the eagerness of their own movement against the current and drawn out of any will to rest by long habit of response to the flashes of the disturbed launce fish. After feeding they lay on the bottom, pressed to the rock as though hiding. The dim light that filtered down was scarcely reflected from their wide backs; they lay at all angles in the sheltered water and only moved to feed again when a shift of current touched them.

In the next dawn they moved on again and for several days after that they worked in stops and starts down along the coast of Graham Island. Somewhere still north of Skidegate Channel they found a fine bank over which the current ran steadily, scarcely affected by the tides. The launce fish were thick there and they fed along the bank in shelter from the stimulation of the current for five days and nights. At the end of that time they had worked up to an exposed place; the sudden force of the current seemed to touch every nerve in their bodies. They headed into it, circled once over the bank, forming into a tight school, then traveled southward without pause for six hours.

Off the south of the Queen Charlottes a heavy mid-March gale met them. It blew in pelting fury from the south, building the current flow to a strong force near the surface. Spring rode up into it, felt it around her, felt the responsive pull of the forces within her. She swam gladly into the wild drive of the big waves, seeking the strongest current. Occasionally she leapt clear out into the stinging spray, falling back heavily on her side to shake the sea-lice from their hold above her anal fin. Around her other fish of the school leapt out, falling back in heavy white splashes that the wind tore instantly from the face of the water. The gale blew for six days and they headed steadily into it, resting seldom. For a few calm days after that they traveled and fed uncertainly fifty or sixty miles to the west of Calvert Island. Then another gale blew up from the open ocean and led them down to Cape Scott and the west coast of Vancouver Island again.

They passed Cape Cook at the end of March and re-found the banks off Barkley Sound during the first week of April. There were launce fish there and Euphausids and the school fed restlessly in shelter from the steady northwestward current, lay in shelter and fed again. The trollers passed over them, fishing slowly, near bottom. Spring fed now with an uncertain savagery, often seizing a small fish and holding it for several minutes across her jaws before relaxing her grip to turn and swallow it. Often she disregarded forage fish when they were within easy reach of her and again at times she drove fiercely to attack them when their distant movement was only a half-seen flicker in the water. A troller's spoons passed well away from her and she swam across to them, followed one a little distance and turned away from it. Spoons passed close to her as she lay on the bottom and she disregarded them. They passed again, so close that one of the heavy leads almost touched her and its passage stirred water and sand about her. She started up sharply, rushed at the nearest spoon and followed it, her nose almost touching the hook. Suddenly she struck at the spoon and held it. The point of the hook met bone in her jaw, slid along it and tore away. A bell jingled wildly on one of Happy Hammond's poles, the spring stretched almost to its fullest and sprang back into a coil again. Happy brought in the line, expecting a break, telling himself he had lost the biggest fish of a couple of seasons.

The power of the current drew them on the next day. For a short while they traveled as a great school of several hundred fish, but the school began to break up almost as it started and when Spring turned down towards the bottom late in the morning only sixty or eighty fish were left with her. Within a week of leaving the banks off Barkley Sound they came to Swiftsure Bank. The school split again, leaving fifteen or twenty fish to turn into the Straits of Juan de Fuca for the Fraser River and Puget Sound. The rest stayed only a short while on the bank and then held southward, once again in a school of several hundred.

Spring had advanced a long way in maturity since leaving the Queen Charlottes. Her eggs were still small and her ovaries had swelled to only a fraction of the length and weight they would reach by September, but she seemed a different fish. Her scales were set more tightly and firmly in the skin of her body and they seemed suddenly larger; there were more than a hundred and twenty concentric rings on each one, showing the growth of five summers and six winters. Her tail seemed squarer, her body color already slightly darker, though she was still a splendid deepsea fish, silver-bellied and with a strong blue-gray translucency above the lateral line. Even now, south of Swiftsure Bank and within a few days of the mouth of her own river, she was not driven by the urgent haste that their swollen ovaries put upon the fall-running fish; but she was firmly meshed by her own development into a machinery of tides and currents and temperatures, perhaps also of pressures and chemical influences, that was drawing and driving her inevitably towards the spawning grounds.

There had been, all through her life, strong physical satisfactions. There had been strong pleasure in feeding to repletion in the Canyon Pool, stronger pleasure of feeding near Astoria and among the massed Euphausids of the ocean, a vibrant ecstasy in driving time after time upon the schools of silver herrings. There had been pleasure in the drive of her muscles through the water, in the free curved leaping that eased the irritation of the sea-lice that held their sucking grip on the tenderest part of her belly, perhaps even a pleasure of speed and strength in the terror of flight from enemies. There was pleasure, or at least an ease of security, in the closeness of other salmon about her, and there had been an ease in the response to conditions within her and around her that led her down her rivers to the sea. But none of these had been strong as the thing that ruled her now. It turned her from feeding, huddled her on the bottom, then flowed into her, stirred her, at once drove her and drew her in a sudden change of current or light. In responding there was pleasure, pleasure of release, delight in the use of her strong body to stem the force of water against her, pleasure in the gradual shifting of pressures and changing of shapes within her body cavity.

Swimming with a great school of maturing chinooks she came back to the influence of the Columbia at the end of April, little more than a hundred days after she had started from the Queen Charlotte Islands. She sensed the changing water when she was still far out and without hesitation turned into it. A good part of the school turned with her and they worked into the cloudy water for some distance before they found a resting place in a deep hole behind a sandbar. There were salmon already in the hole when they came there and others came after them. There were the fish of several different years there, from a few seven-year-olds down to two-year-old jacks, and there were fish of all sizes, from great broad-sided creatures a full foot longer than Spring and weighing eighty or ninety pounds down to the precociously maturing jacks which weighed two pounds or less. Near Spring at all times in her migration was the fish that had been tagged with her. A little ahead of her in the hole there lay a great eighty-pound male, Sachem, of the summer hog-run that passes above Rock Island. To one side of her was a second male, smaller than the first but still well over fifty pounds—Chinook, a fish from the Snake River. Fish moved restlessly at all times in the hole, but these four and a few others with them seemed a school within the school and when one of them moved the others moved also, rising into mid-water, circling, settling down to the bottom again.

The trollers knew the rest hole and worked over it diligently with slow deep spoons. The maturing fish were hard to move, but in the short periods about slack water and change of light they lifted from the bottom to circle restlessly or change position, and at those times many of them were caught. The spoons passed close to Spring many times and usually, when she was poised above bottom, she turned towards them or sometimes followed a little way. The school was completing a restless circle at faint daylight when Sachem struck. The spoon drew across his tail, wobbling with tempting slowness inches before Spring's eyes. Sachem turned sharply upon it with a mighty flash of his broad body and was traveling at speed against its direction when he seized it. The shock of his take against the weight of the boat jumped the heavy lead sharply away from the bottom. The troller's strong cuttyhunk leader parted a few feet from the spoon but Sachem rode on up, still fighting his battle with the sharp pain in his jaw and the six-inch drag of metal he could not shake from him. He rode to the surface in the full drive of his strength and broke water in an echoing leap. He broke again and again, slamming down on side or belly each time so that white spray flew high about him. The troller watched, his lines untended, his foot on the tiller circling the boat to get a closer view of what he had lost. Sachem leapt a dozen times, until he was tired and some of the fury had left him. Then he went down again and lay in his old position a little ahead of Spring, the bright spoon showing clearly against the bottom at the head of his dim outline.

The clumsy spoon-bait in his jaw increased Sachem's restlessness. He would lie for an hour or more without moving, then start up into the water in a violent twisting rush that sometimes took him clear up to the surface and out in a head-shaking leap. The passing and repassing of the trolling boats, the struggles of hooked fish, the movement of other schools through the hole combined with Sachem's violence to disturb Spring and the rest of the school immediately about her. They moved on an ebb tide, traveling strongly against the double flow of tide and river to another sheltered place only a little short of the bar.

This resting place was known and fished by anglers as well as by commercial trollers. Spoons and spinners, hook-mounted herrings, plugs and wobblers of all types drew past the fish almost constantly from dawn till dark. Spring had already stopped feeding—her body was in prime condition, stored with strength to form her eggs to the full size and supply her with energy for the ascent to the spawning grounds; and in the steadily moving changes within her, her stomach was contracting so that it no longer drove her to seek food. But the movement of the baits in the water near her was often a danger. The sight of their halting flight struck through her eyes to nerves and senses and muscles conditioned through five years to instant pursuit and capture of whatever small thing moved within reach. At times she was beyond all reach of temptation to strike; lying on the bottom, solidly immobile, she scarcely saw what passed her. Then, stirred by flow of current or change of light or both together, she would be poised, vibrant with the sudden stimulation, ready to follow and perhaps to strike.

At such times were hooked most of the salmon that the fishermen took from that resting place. Generally the big fish, Spring among them, moved slowly in pursuit, so slowly that the fifteen-pounders and often the tiny male jacks were ahead of them. But once a red-and-white plug crossed Spring so closely that she had only to move a few inches and open her jaws to suck it into her. The angler raised his rod sharply at the pull and the front gang hook took precarious hold in the point of her upper jaw. As lightly hooked fish sometimes will, Spring became a fury of action. She ran swiftly, first down, then up towards the surface where she broke in a slash of white water. Even in the break she kept running, turning in a wide half-circle that left the drowned line marking her course. She leapt twice, her body half out of the water, then clear out so that the weight of the drowned line flung tail over head in a somersault that broke the hookhold. Free of it she sounded back to the hole, to lie in temporary exhaustion behind great Sachem. As she lay there Sachem struggled again, head down and tail far up in the water. The hook that held the spoon in his jaw dropped almost easily from its loose hold in the two-inch gash his runs had torn; the spoon lay on the bottom of the hole, shining dimly against the sand that had already begun to cover it.

The school moved up and began to work into the mouth of the river during the first few days of May. Their progress from resting place to resting place and from the last resting place towards the bar had not been straightforward; they had turned back upon themselves several times, swimming always into the tide, towards the river mouth on the ebb, often almost directly away from it on the flood. Only by the balance of the constant river current over the even match of ebb and flow did they make way towards the bar, and by the same balance, made greater now by the confinement of the river, they finally crossed the bar and entered the estuary. The wind was southeasterly as they crossed and it held southeasterly for several days, drawing them over towards the Oregon side.

They moved slowly upstream, still turning to meet each flood and traveling some way down against it before the ebb returned, but in little more than a week they were above Astoria and away from the brackish

water. The Columbia was coming up to its spring
freshet, with the weight of melting snows behind it
pouring half a million cubic feet of fresh water seawards
every second. Spring met the flow gladly, forcing herself into it with a new energy behind Sachem's great
tail; to right of her and a little ahead Chinook swam
easily towards Idaho; close alongside her the second
tagged fish from her own river held steadily; around
this group a great mixed school of spring-run chinooks
moved in shifting formation like a flight of geese.

## Chapter Sixteen

THE school with which Spring traveled had entered
the river at a fortunate time. They were later than
the main spring run and still ahead of the summer fish,
so that the net fishery was less intense than it would
have been a short while earlier or would become later
on. Then too, the river was running in good volume,
giving them wider and deeper channels to follow; and
the stationary traps of the Oregon side were still only
complicated clusters of piling—the power of the river,
carrying the spring weight of snags and small debris,
has taught the trap fishermen that they cannot hold
their web until the flow slackens in July.

Below Astoria the fish had been among floating gill-
nets and near occasional haul seines; twice, swimming
near bottom, the whole school had passed under the lead

lines of drifting gill-nets, but they had not once been touched or turned. As they went on there were more nets, nearly all of them gill-nets, but gill-nets of many types and kinds. A few were simple floating nets, quarter-mile lengths of mesh wide enough to let the front part of a salmon's body pass through, narrow enough to tangle gill covers and pectorals when he tried to draw back from the touch of the twine. These hung almost invisibly in the roiled water, stretching twenty or thirty feet down from the cork line at the surface. Many more were diver nets, with heavy lead lines carefully balanced to draw the cork line down below the surface yet not to anchor the net to bottom, so that the whole net carried downstream through the drift of a set with lead line touching sand. Within these main types the nets varied again, reflecting the infinite variation of skill, experience, ingenuity and whim of the men who fished them. Some were simple, depending only upon matching the size of mesh to size of fish for their effectiveness; others were double curtains, with narrower mesh on the upstream side so that the smaller fish that passed through the wide mesh would be caught; other double nets had a downstream curtain of fine-meshed gill-net while the upstream curtain was a heavy wide-meshed trammel through which big fish could drag a bag of the fine net and become trapped in a closed purse. Sometimes yet another net was hung on the downstream side of these, stretched between cork line and a very light lead line so that the current held it out like a lean-to roof, to catch fish that turned up and sought to go over the main net.

Altogether more than a thousand gill-nets fished the Columbia, from more than a thousand boats. The boats, like the nets, had steadily developed to a greater efficiency through nearly ninety years of fishing experience. When Spring ran to the river most of them were twenty-five or thirty feet long, powered with good engines and skillfully designed to give every aid to speed and ease in handling the nets. A great many were one-man boats, built with a set of controls in the bow and live rollers over which the fisherman could easily bring in his net singlehanded; all could drift through a set, take in the net and plug upstream to the head of the drift again in only a fraction of the time taken by boats of earlier days.

If the sum of this efficiency was a threat to Spring and her race, it was also a justification for their survival. Year after year the drift gill-nets take their millions of pounds of chinooks in the Columbia and men live by it, fairly and freely—fishermen, packers, cannery workers and the men who supply these people with their daily needs and the men who sell the salmon in the cans. It builds a solid block of human life dependent upon the salmon runs and determined that nothing—unless it be too much fishing and canning—shall destroy them utterly. So, running the gauntlet of nets in her upstream passage, Spring was at the fullest point of her relationship with mankind—if she struck a net and became en-

tangled she would purchase by her death some brief
fraction of the livelihood of several men; if she escaped
to the spawning grounds she would breed other fish to
return, or fail to return, through the same barriers to
the same purpose.

Above Tongue Point, as they drew away from the
strongest influence of the tides, the upstream progress
of the chinooks became more rapid. Entering the river
and for a little way inside the mouth Spring and the
fish traveling with her had advanced less than a mile a
day, since they swam through long hours against each
flood tide. But with each day's advance the next day's
speed became greater and by the time they reached
Puget Island it had risen to four or five miles a day.
They followed the channel to southward of the Island,
where the steep dark-green hills of the Oregon side run
down to the smoke and naked timber stacks of the sawmills and the little ferry plies across in hourly trips to
Westport. The school felt its passing through the water
as they passed and Sachem slowly turned a little down
from the vibration; the others followed. On the deck of
the ferry a fisherman talked to a tourist, looking back
towards the double-ended gill-net boats tied near the
slip.

"No," he said. "Gill-netting isn't what it used to be.
I've been at it thirty years and made pretty good sometimes, but there's nothing in it now."

The tourist said: "They told us up at Bonneville that
a record run of fish was going through the ladders."

"Yeah? I hadn't heard that. The boys here reckon it's been the worst season for years. It's early yet and we could have missed some fish, I guess—the channels change some and a fellow don't always get on to 'em early in the year. But I think she's going down and down all the time."

The tourist nodded. "Looks kind of dead, all right. We didn't see many boats fishing between here and Longview."

The fisherman's attitude seemed to change. He straightened from the rail, then leaned his elbows on it again. "That don't mean much. Spring run's pretty near over right now and the boys ain't out there. She'll pick up plenty when the later fish come in." He shifted again, watching the slip near the lumber yard as the ferry came near the end of its short run. "I was talking to a guy the other day who reckoned the runs might get a whole lot better. His angle was that these big dams, like Bonneville and them, don't do no harm because they've been figured out for fish. And with putting in the big dams the Fisheries guys have got wise to all the small dams and the irrigation ditches and all them hay-wire things that was doing real harm and have made the guys that own 'em fix 'em up right for fish. Might be something to it, too. It's a cinch they listen to the fisherman more than they used to do."

The ferry ground her iron-shod nose against the piles that led her to the slip and the tourist turned towards his car. Up the channel Spring and Chinook and the school of salmon swam on behind Sachem's slow and cautious lead. He searched the strongest current of the deepest channels, working his strong body through the water in easy movement that slid from shoulder to back on through the less massive part of his body to his great tail, then rippled again down the same length of muscle and bone and scales. He seemed to probe the cloudy water ahead of him, suspicious of danger; actually he swam slowly in strong sense of security and in sensual pleasure at the flow of fresh water through mouth and gills and along his sides. So he came slowly against the net. It was a diver net, small-mesh gill web in front and heavy trammel behind. He felt the small-mesh, pushed at it with his nose, then turned and swam along it. Spring and the other fish turned with him. Spring felt his uneasiness within her as surely as though she herself had touched the web and she was prime for panic, ready to drive through the water in frantic flight at any warning.

Sachem worked uneasily along the web, turning from time to time to thrust his nose against it, loath to turn quite away, downstream. The school followed, some of those nearest the web matching his movements. A two-pound jack, driven as surely as the others by the milt precociously developing in his body cavity, turned in and found a way through the narrow web and through the trammel. A fifteen-pound fish tried to follow him. Its body wedged in the narrow mesh a little ahead of the dorsal fin; it struggled, jerking the unseen net corks above, tried to draw back and gilled. It was the warning for which the school had waited. The nearest fish turned sharply away. The movement spread; more fish turned, Spring turned, Chinook turned, Sachem turned and they were away downstream.

Within a few yards the flight slowed. Within a hundred yards it turned. The school re-formed and Sachem led them slowly well up in the water, then forward again, into the current at the old questing pace. They passed high above the cork line of the net as it drifted along its set and were free in the current once more.

The school held on its journey through the broad lower reaches of the river, past the farms that used the narrow flatlands on the banks, past sloughs where booms of logs rested for mile after mile in the teredo-free water, past the low islands which grew cottonwoods and alders and spruces and yet more farms, past a hundred gill-nets drifting along channels that tight groups of fishermen had cleared of snags and debris. Automobile traffic raced along roads on either side of the river and saw nothing of salmon except the gray net-boats distant in the lapping gray water. Freighters passed on their way to and from Portland and Vancouver, tugs and barges and log booms passed, but few even of these saw salmon. Spring and Chinook and Sachem and the other fish with them held on their way well down in deep channels by day; at night they lay a great deal in shallow water, often very close to the shore; and sometimes briefly in the early dawn their passing was marked on the face of a smooth river by the gently pushing arrowhead ripples that had shown the passing of their ancestors; occasionally one of them jumped, always upstream, over in an arc to enter the water head first again; sometimes, especially towards dusk, they broke water in slow rolling that showed first nose, then wide, wet, gleaming back and dorsal fin, and last the broad strong tail.

They passed under Longview Bridge at dawn and by dusk were more than six miles upstream. Three days later Spring began to taste the pollution of the river she must follow to find her own stream. The whole school still held together, well over near the Oregon shore, but it was already shaping into two schools. Spring and the tagged fish near her had swung a little from their places behind Sachem and Chinook and all through the school there had been a gradual shifting and forming and re-forming. That evening the two schools did separate. The smaller school, in which Spring was, turned away towards the bank, then swung in a wide circle and came up behind the larger school. Both schools lay quietly and close together in the shallow eddy through the night and they started on together at the next dawn. But gradually and with frequent returning they won free of the thing that held them together and at last they lost each other. Sachem and Chinook and the fish behind them held on in the full glow of the main river, towards Bonneville and the still far-distant streams that had bred them. Spring left the Columbia, facing into the pollution through which she had so hardly come as a yearling.

The year was late and the snows of Spring's valley still clung to the high hillsides, but the polluted river was running with cleaner, fresher flow than when Spring had come down it. She passed again among the sewers and wharves and piling of the great city and felt again the stir of its shipping. Against the strong straight force of water above the last complication of tide she traveled faster and more steadily. The school was tempted again and again as it rested by the flashes of wobbling spoons and plugs and lures of many kinds, and from time to time a fish stirred angrily, struck to kill the thing that passed too close and was hooked by some happy angler. Spring was close to this danger many times, but her shrunken stomach had weaned her from overquick response to the invitation of weak movement, and generally she lay quite still while the bait hung near her. Once, soon after she was clear of the city, a jointed plug sank down in the water and touched her. She moved away from it slightly, not more than enough to let it pass. The current carried it the length of her body and several feet beyond, then slowly, rising a little, it drew back past her. Several times it passed and repassed along her length, then hung, slowly swaying as the current sent lifelike ripples through its body, just behind her tail. Spring held to the bottom, fully aware of it, for perhaps five minutes. Then she stirred, moved a little upstream, swung in a sharp circle and came in behind it.

For a little while she watched it, her nose within a few inches of the tail hook. The plug moved up a little, not more than a foot. Spring matched the movement, opened her jaws and closed them gently on it. In his anchored boat the angler was half asleep. It was nearly thirty seconds before he noticed that the movement of his plug was no longer gently throbbing through line and rod-top. Even as she opened her jaws and released the plug Spring saw it start suddenly away from her, rising swiftly through the water in upstream flight. She settled back to the bottom. In the boat the angler examined his plug and shook his head. "Must have been weed," he said.

## Chapter Seventeen

Sachem and Chinook held on their way up the Columbia with a big school of spring-run fish all about them. It was still a conglomerate school, headed for several different spawning tributaries, and they were very much above the average size of the fish in it. Most of these were close to the May average of fifteen or twenty pounds; a few, early fish of the summer hog-run that comes to Rock Island on the tail of the spring run, were over thirty pounds. But, except only great Sachem, there was hardly a fish there weighing within ten pounds of Chinook's full fifty. Both Sachem and Chinook were exceptional fish. Chinook had left his nursery stream in the Snake watershed early in his first year and was returning after five vigorous years of feeding that had taken him to the north coast of the Queen Charlottes, well beyond the limit of Spring's long feeding range. Sachem was a year older and had traveled farther still, though he had spent part of his first year in a tributary stream above Grand Coulee; nearly six years of ocean life had carried him to a point off the southern coast of Alaska and built his body to its present huge size. Later in the year a few other fish like him would be running the big waters of the Columbia to seek spawning room far up the Snake or in streams that the insurmountable mass of Grand Coulee dam now blocked from all salmon. There might be a few, very few, even larger, weighing perhaps ninety, perhaps a hundred pounds; but Sachem was a true giant of his species.

As the school passed through the middle reaches of the river towards Bonneville they came upon more nets. Above Portland the river reaches back into the beginning of the Cascade Range, flowing with impressive width between mountain-high banks of green timber and bald rock faces. From a distance it seems a smooth flow, serene and magnificent in sweeping breadth. Go down to the level of the water and there are waves lapping at the sandy beaches, white-flecked water whirled and murmuring over bars, smooth strong glides in deep channels, little upstream curving wavelets in the creased water behind the upthrust of big rocks. In the vastness, beyond river size, the power of each showing is deceptively reduced, but it is there, the power of a hundred rivers, a thousand streams, a hundred thousand creeks whose headwaters lie as far east as the summit of the Rockies, separated from the sources of the Mississippi and the Saskatchewan only by a few yards of granite.

Only a little above Reed Island the fish met another gill-net. It was a diver-net, drifting along a channel between the sandbars in a good flow of current. The school had started upstream from their shallow resting place of the night before less than an hour earlier and they were traveling steadily against the good current. A little below the net the passing of a tugboat disturbed a few fish near the outside of the school; they swung in, swimming fast; the movement spread to the other fish and reached Sachem almost as he came to the net. He started forward in a panicky rush, struck the eight-and-a-half-inch mesh at full speed and tore through the single curtain as though it were not there at all. Chinook, close behind him, burst the web again before it was well back of his head and several fish slipped through the holes the big fish had left. A few gilled but many more passed safely outside the net, for the school had struck only a few yards from the buoyed end.

They came to the tail of the strong race below Bonneville Dam less than a week after passing Vancouver. It was a clear day with a strong sun that lighted the little houses of the village and the great concrete structures of the dam to brilliant whiteness. Men still worked on the powerhouse to the south of Bradford Island and only a single one of the twenty-three-foot runners turned in its draft tube, five revolutions in each four seconds, shedding a tiny part of the Columbia's flow into electricity. The rest of the mounting spring might of the river roared in increasing thunder through a dozen gates of the spillway dam north of the island. The water came under the steel gates, driven by a forty-foot head to shoot out and upward in solid, glassy, curving streams that broke over in savage crests of heavy tumbled whiteness ten feet higher than the foot of each gate. The crests broke again, fell back on themselves, fountained up in spires of water, gathered themselves and crashed on in steep waves that made a white rapid of fierce water for more than a mile below the dam.

Sachem and Chinook came into this gladly. The growing strength of the broken current called to their own strength, its tossing thrust against them wakened every driving muscle of their great bodies and they fought up steadily, almost swiftly, wide tails forcing the racing water behind them in swirling strokes of power. As the current grew stronger and wilder the school broke up, each fish striving on its own. Sachem and Chinook remained together almost side by side. Little by little the solid strength of the water and the battering uncertainty of its flow began to slow them. Two or three hundred feet below the gates they swung over towards Bradford Island, seeking an easier flow. They found shelter behind a big rock near shore and rested briefly. Then Sachem drove out into the current again and Chinook still followed him closely. They forced up strongly at first and Sachem leapt out once, his huge wide body dark and clear against the shattered whiteness. The full strength of the race caught them and slowed them again until they were moving foot by foot, then inch by inch. For a full minute they struggled side by side, near the surface, barely holding place, then sharply slacked the effort. The current carried them back and they turned down and found shelter to the side and near bottom. Again they rested only briefly; the rush of the current above them was a summons and they turned up into it. They quartered across, making headway, then swung back, still quartering. Brilliant light water was all about them, full of bubbles and foam, some of its strength lost in the breaking but giving only a light purchase for the thrust of their tails and the drive of their bodies. Sachem rolled his back out, so that it shone black in the sun and whiteness, then went down; Chinook followed him. Together they met the solid wall of water that forced under the gate, plunged into it, almost held; then it caught them up, hurled them over, tumbled them, battered them, threw them back down the race. They won out of it and slid suddenly into a quieter flow close against Bradford Island.

There were other fish in the smooth water and for a little while Sachem and Chinook rested there quietly. Sachem stirred at last, swam up to the surface and rolled once. He felt the current there, smooth and easy but strong enough to draw him. He slid forward into it, sought its changing direction between concrete walls, felt it suddenly strong and had found his way into the Bradford Island ladder. Chinook followed a little behind him.

The ladder was a curving quarter-mile length of fast-flowing water that drew down across the island from the slough behind the powerhouse. It was cut into wide pools by six-foot walls of concrete over which the surface water flowed to join the race of the spillway and draw the salmon from it as their struggle in the heavy current wearied them. Sachem, holding near surface, came against the first wall and turned down from it to the concrete bottom of the ladder. A moment later he turned sharply upward and came out of the water in a curving leap that carried him over the wall and into the first pool of the ladder. Chinook was deeper in the water as he came up and felt a strong flow of current near one of the walls of the fishway; he held into it, swam easily through a wide opening in the cross wall of the first pool, turned to follow the draw of current and was beside Sachem again.

The two fish worked up together from pool to pool in the bright water. The entrances were square gaps cut near bottom in the concrete cross walls of the ladder, alternating from left to right in each pool. A strong flow slid through the gaps against each solid wall opposite, then along well under the surface current to pass out through the lower gap to the next pool. The fish followed its turns easily, resting when they wanted in the eddying water of the pools, seldom near surface. Other fish passed up with them, chinooks, a few steelhead, lampreys, suckers and some squawfish. The steelhead were restless and quick, their square tails forcing even more vigorously through the water than those of the chinooks; quite often they jumped instead of passing through the underwater gaps, and one of them, in panic or excess of energy, jumped wildly many times, striking the side wall of the ladder, smashing down into the rush of white water on the surface, sometimes falling back over the step he had gained. He grew calmer at last and passed up with the others, silently and invisibly through the easy force of the gaps.

Sachem came at last to a steel grating across the ladder. He felt his way along it, pressing his nose to the narrow openings where the water came through, seeking a way to follow on into the current. He worked gently and persistently back and forth along the grating for several minutes; once or twice he pressed his nose tight against the bars and thrust with a tentative wriggle of tail and body as though trying their strength. At last he turned back and disappeared into the deep water of the pool. Other fish, Chinook among them, came up and searched for a way through the heavy grating. They turned away, came back, turned away again, swimming with calm, patient movements.

The grating was set across the ladder only a few steps below its entrance into Bradford Slough. In the center there was a heavy wooden hatch-door, tight closed. On the upstream side of this was a white plate set a few inches under the water and flanked by two little sentry boxes with forward-slanting glass windows that looked down on the plate. It seemed quiet there at the counting station, away from the roar of the spillway, and a little group of tourists stood watching the fish at the grating, seeing the green-roofed sentry boxes against the orange California poppies growing on the raw gravel bank thrown up behind them. A counter came down, passed among the tourists without a word and settled himself in one of the boxes. He opened the gate and almost at once a fish slipped through, then another, two out of perhaps half a million that would pass that way during the year.

Sachem and Chinook were resting deep in the pool when the gate was opened. The stir of other fish passing through moved them and they came up to the grating again, worked along it, found the opening, turned away, came back. Sachem crept forward cautiously, wriggling his great body until his head was over the white plate. The tourists watched and called to each other and pointed. Even the man in the counting house moved forward a little on his stool to get a better sight of Sachem's great body, dim against the dark water of the pool. Sachem moved forward until his pectorals came over the plate, then the bright light reflecting from the white surface was too much for him and he turned sharply and fled into the depths of the pool. Chinook obeyed the warning of his panic, but in a little while the two fish came back, still swimming slowly and cautiously. Sachem's head came over the plate again, then his pectorals, then his dorsal fin, breaking the surface. Chinook moved up almost in his shadow, his own wide head small beside the widest part of Sachem's huge body. Sachem's full length came over the plate and for a brief moment was sharply there against the white reflection; a dozen pairs of human eyes made the brief sight their own, for all time; the spread pectorals sensitive and almost delicate, the huge width of the back, the full length of the mighty body, dorsal fin and tip of tail dark and gleaming above water in the sunlight, head tapered and graceful from bulky shoulder. Then it was gone. Sachem slid off the plate into the dark water of the next pool. Chinook followed him. The counter glanced quickly up at the tourists and smiled, accepting them for a brief moment as equals who would understand, then turned back to his watching.

The two fish passed quickly and easily up through the remaining steps and out into the slough. They searched and found the easy flow of current to the turbine under the south bank, followed against it a little way, then turned to rest in an eddy below the mouth of Eagle Creek.

Other fish were in the eddy and more came to it. In a little while a new school formed and went on.

Above Bonneville the river is narrow and deep right up to Cascade Locks, where the legendary span of the

Bridge of the Gods is a mass of tumbled sunken rock clear across the bed of the river. In spite of the dam there is a fine current through the reach and the school delayed only long enough to rest after climbing the ladder. One day later they were through the strong run of the cascades and well into the wide glassy curve where the banks of the river change from the moist green of the coast to the buff and gray rock-pierced sand of the interior. The gray cone of Wind Mountain, tremendous with rock on its upstream face, looked down on their passing and the Washington streams, Wind River and the White Salmon Rivers, drew fish from the school until Hood River came down from Oregon, draining the snows from the ridge-veined face of tall Mount Hood. Even here, a hundred and fifty miles from salt water, there were nets, but Sachem and Chinook passed safely among them and came safely to the Dalles, where the river confines its breadth in depth as it slides brimming through a flume of lava two hundred feet high and a stone's throw wide.

They worked up the main channel, shouldering the water behind them in the slow crescendo of their upstream movement. At Bonneville they had left the last slight influence of ocean tide and now they were free in the full fresh force of the river, facing strong clean flow or tumbled rapids for mile after mile as the river wound among the dry hills with their lava ramparts gaunt and black against burnt green.

Above the Dalles, almost a part of them still, is Celilo

Falls. Sachem and Chinook came late to the falls, several weeks late in the year they ran. At Celilo Falls the Indians fish as they fished before any white men had seen the Columbia, raking the salmon with dip-nets from the eddies below the steep drop of the water. When they fish the river is low and pours down over the rock in varying heights from its different channels; the salmon lie in the eddies at such times, jumping out a great deal as though seeking an easy way over the obstacle; they search through the white water under the falls and around the wooden supports of the platforms on which the Indians stand to fish, and they cross from eddy to eddy. The long-handled dip-nets plunge and lift, probing and searching deep in the water; they pass among salmon, touch salmon to panic, lift salmon to death. But only at low water. Each year there is a race towards Celilo Falls from two directions—the speed of the year in the snows descending from the hills of the headwaters against the speed of the ascending spring run of chinooks. When the heavy waters are first, as they were in the year Sachem and Chinook ran, Celilo Falls is only a fierce run of backward-curving waves on the river's face and the Indians must wait till summer for their fish.

Above Celilo there are no nets and little fishing of any sort. As they passed along the big island that splits the river above the falls and felt the swift flow of the Deschutes River's entrance, Sachem and Chinook seemed safe fish, within certain reach of their spawning.

## CHAPTER EIGHTEEN

SPRING moved steadily up the polluted river until she came near the horseshoe dam above the two great mills. Where the strong flow of water came from the turbines of the mill on the left bank she sought a way up, but at first could find none and so turned to rest in the pool formed by the tailrace.

A school of about a dozen fish had come with her into the pool and there were others already there. There were also spoon-baits and spinners hanging in the water, holding place almost steadily, moved only by the force of the current while the fishermen waited in their boats under the shade of great, colored umbrellas. The second tagged fish had remained constantly with Spring all through her ascent of the river and now lay close beside her in the pool. A spoon hung above them, wobbling light flashes in endless succession, now sinking a little, now rising a little in the water as tricks of current caught it. The tagged fish moved very suddenly up through the water, seized it and began a long downstream run. The fisherman jerked up from the shade of his umbrella, held hard and in a little while had checked the run. The fish came back up the pool fast, felt the line slack and sounded; at the bottom he rested with his tail well up, his head down on the boulders, swimming gently to hold the position. The fisherman tightened on him at last, pulled and hauled and lifted, but could not move him. He waited and tried again, then again, without success. At last he raised his anchor and let the boat drift down in the stream. The fish felt the line slack, then the pull from downstream shifted him. He started to run upstream, was turned and came down close to the boat. The angler leaned over, gaff in hand, and the metal of the tag against the dark tail caught his eye. He strained to lift the fish within reach, struck overanxiously with the gaff and watched his fish run again upstream in a rush that almost tore the rod from his hands. He was an old man and the fight had already exhausted him; his fingers tried clumsily to check his racing reel and prevent the backlash, but could not. The line came tight, the rod drew down almost to the water, and the hook tore away. Sadly the old man let his boat drift on in the current.

The tagged fish was no longer with Spring when she moved up out of the pool, seeking a way to follow her journey. She searched the tailrace again, moving up and down and from side to side in the strongest current, but there was no way through. At last she swung into the big eddy to rest; crossing it she felt a light flow and she followed that, very slowly, right up through the wide stretch of slack water inside the curve of the dam. The flow held her near surface and as she went up it grew in strength until it brought her to its fall from a salmon ladder cut in the solid rock of the old falls. It was a little narrow way compared to the great ladders at Bonneville, but the water that flowed from it, freshened by the fall through the steps, had a strong call for Spring. She circled twice where the bubbles danced in the dark still water of the unused spillway, went down deep, then came up with a rush that carried her over the lip of the first step.

The steps were cut on alternate sides to half their width and depth, so that each had a rush of water through the low side and an eddy behind the high side. Spring passed up the ladder almost without resting, sometimes jumping from one step to another, sometimes swimming through the rush of water. Other fish came up the ladder close behind her and a small school formed to travel on above the dam.

For more than a week they worked up the gentle river among the soft farm lands, past the quiet stir of early haymaking, past the heart of the valley in the loveliest city of all Oregon, back towards the distant hills and dark-green timber. Spring found and followed the flow of her own stream when she was still far from its mouth. She held to it persistently and when she turned into its rocky channel from the main stream she was following an only course rather than making a turn. The feel of the water, its temperature, flow, its whole analysis matched desire and want and need that was deep in her flesh, unsatisfied till then in every pulse of her living. She swam gladly against it among a dozen other fish that had turned with her and they mounted steadily through pool and rapid for five or six miles to a broad shallow where many other chinooks were collected.

The fish near the shallow were nervous and restless. Many hung below in slightly deeper water, working up from time to time, then splashing down to circle and come up again. They moved almost constantly in small schools and often the sudden panicky splashing of ten or a dozen of them would startle a hundred or more until the water was churned and splashed all across the stream by the thresh of tails against the surface. The nervousness communicated itself to Spring and the other fish near her immediately, but she swam up on to the shallow and sought to pass over it. So she came to the rack.

It stretched right across the river, a line of sturdy tripods, built of cedar poles and heavily weighted with rocks. Spring could work up under these, but there were wooden slats nailed an inch or two apart on the upstream side, slanting forward down into the gravel. A great number of chinooks held close to this barrier, feeling the flow of current between the slats, sometimes testing them as Sachem had tested the iron bars of the grating at Bonneville. It was raining and the river had begun to rise so that the urgency of their waiting grew. Spring circled down into the deep water, worked up over the shallow again and found herself facing the barrier at another point. She began to work along it systematically, pushing among the other fish, probing with her nose at the gravel and the slanting wood that held her back.

Senator Evans came down to the rack towards evening. He had been there every day since the salmon had begun to collect below it and now he walked straight out along the narrow board platform to the place from which he knew he could best see the fish. It was still raining, but he sat down on the board and settled himself with his back against one leg of a tripod. A group of fish, disturbed by his coming, fled downstream with nervous splashing; in a little while he saw them working up towards him again.

He sat quite still in his chosen place, watching the fish intently, moving his head little, his blue eyes much. But for all its intentness his watching seemed to lack the enthusiasm and rich satisfaction of his watching from beside the rock wall at the Canyon Pool. His thin shoulders were hunched forward under his gray coat and the long lines of his thin brown face were deeply drawn; neither his mouth nor his eyes smiled. Once or twice he looked up towards the bank, then back to the fish again. Don Gunner had promised to come down on his way to town and join him at the rack.

Spring worked along under his feet, still searching a way between the slats, but he did not see her. He watched the fish downstream of him and wondered why he minded so much. In a way it didn't really matter; there was the big flat-bottomed scow tied to the far bank and they would come and gather the fish into that, take them up to the ponds, hold them to ripeness and strip the eggs from them. The result probably wouldn't be much less good than natural spawning and it might be better. He thought of the cost and weighed it against the acres of good spawning ground upstream, but he knew that was not what disturbed him, though it had some weight. For sixty years he had watched the salmon pass up to the Canyon Pool. Season after season he had seen their great bodies swaying in the deep shaded rest pools through the summer. He had known his father's delight in their coming and going and had learned some of his own delight from that. The salmon were the river, they were the country, of it and helping to make it. In words, he told himself, it becomes meaningless, merely sentimental. But you can feel it, know that this is right, the other wrong. The river is there for their use, they are its yield, growing from it, growing on it, giving themselves back to it in a cycle that no mere human farming has yet been able to match.

Above the sound of the river he heard a car coming along the rough road from the highway. The engine stopped and Gunner came out on the bank. The old man forgot his thoughts and was smiling and easy. Gunner came along the plank walk and sat beside him. The Senator waved a hand toward the fish.

"There they are, Don. Hundreds of the poor devils. When will they be down after them?"

"Not for several days. They've got some trouble up at the ponds, I believe."

Spring passed under their feet again but neither of them noticed the metal tag in her tail; the rain broke the surface of the water and made it difficult to see the individual fish clearly.

The old man said: "I went over to Bonneville the other day. It does a man's heart good to see that place."

Gunner looked at him and smiled. "The fish or the power?"

"Both," the old man said. "I've wanted for more than half my life to see that power used, to see it go out to the people who need it. Now I can see that. But I've been afraid always that it would mean the end of the fish. Now I've seen the power taken and the fish going through as well as they ever could. And I tell you, Don, it's a good thing, a grand thing in America."

Gunner nodded. "It's a good job," he said. "They didn't have the time really, but they made a good job. It's all a good job as far as the salmon are concerned; I'm more and more sure of that. You've never seen what they're doing at Rock Island, have you?"

"To compensate for Grand Coulee, you mean? No, I haven't, but I'm going there sometime. I've wanted to ever since I first heard about it. Getting old, Don; homebound."

"I've got to go over in a couple of weeks' time. Why not come along?"

"I'll do that."

"Fine. I'll give you a call about it. I'll have to go now —got to be in Salem tonight. Don't brood too much about your own chinooks. The hatchery boys will look after them for you."

The Senator looked up and smiled. "You shouldn't mock at such a gray old man, Don." He looked down at the fish again. "Say, Don. Do you remember what this year is?"

Don turned back and shook his head. "No," he said. "What is it?"

"It's the fifth year since I marked those fingerlings in the Canyon Pool—the last year any of them are likely to show up."

"Hell, that's right. I'm sorry. Maybe we wouldn't have seen anything, but it was a nice experiment and I'd have liked to see it get a chance." He started to go on, then turned back. "Tell you one thing, though. With the hatchery picking them all up we'll have whatever chance there is of finding the marked fish that Charlie Wilson reported tagging a year or two ago."

The old man stayed on the rack after he had gone. It was still raining, getting dusk; he stood up on the plank and looked back upstream. He reached forward and put his hand on one of the slats. He looked behind him, furtively, towards each bank, then pulled hard on the slat. It did not move and he took his hands away and stood there, laughing at himself. "Like a thief in the night to set them free," he said. "If only I had that wrecking bar in the basement."

He leaned forward again, watching the water, the drift of leaves and small debris that packed against the rack. A south wind found its way along the river, passed over him and shook the wet leaves of the alders and maples in a gust that flung heavy drops from them. The old man turned and went back along the plank walk. As he reached the bank and started to go up towards his car he paused to read through the notice posted at the end of the walk.

## WARNING

### THE FISH COMMISSION OF THE
### STATE OF OREGON
#### AND THE
### BUREAU OF FISHERIES OF THE UNITED STATES

are authorized by law to erect traps, racks or other obstructions across any of the streams of the State of Oregon for the purpose of obtaining SALMON for propagation purposes, and it shall be unlawful for any person or persons to injure or destroy any such traps, racks, or other obstructions by any means whatever or to take, kill, destroy, or molest any salmon within two (2) miles below any such trap, rack, or other obstruction across any stream of the State of Oregon.

ANY PERSON OR PERSONS GUILTY OF VIOLATING THIS LAW SHALL BE FINED FROM $50.00 TO $1000.00 OR BY IMPRISONMENT IN THE COUNTY JAIL NOT LESS THAN TWENTY-FIVE DAYS NOR MORE THAN ONE YEAR, OR BY BOTH SUCH FINE AND IMPRISONMENT.

FISH COMMISSION.

Through the night the wind grew, sweeping warmly up the river, driving the rain before it up the valley to the tall mountains where the snow still hung. The river sang more strongly over the shallows and, rising, rippled against the bars of the rack. Spring swung back, still seeking a way up against the swelling flow that drew her with more and more violent urgency.

## Chapter Nineteen

Above Celilo Falls in freshet time the Columbia carries half a million cubic feet of water each second through sagebrush dryness of hills and flats. Sometimes there are green farms on little strips of level land near the river and sometimes willows grow along the banks, with poplars darker green among them. Rarely a settlement holds precariously among irrigated cherry orchards. But for mile upon mile there is dry grass and tumbleweed and rabbit-haunted sagebrush, and the dry sand blows over it in the winds of the valley.

The river flows strong and deep through the dryness, encircling flat islands, washing sand and black rock, carrying its flood broadly in creases and folds and little whispering whirlpools, guiding the salmon against it to their spawning. Sachem and Chinook worked steadily towards the big bend where the river leaves the Oregon boundary and turns straight northward through Washington. It is rugged country, fit to bend a great river, light brown and steep, slashed with the black lava, sometimes bold-faced with it, then sloping fast from the face through five hundred or a thousand feet to the water's edge in a torrent of broken blackness released by a thousand years of wind and weather. The hills are flat-topped from the leveled flowing of the lava; and the reflecting surface of the river, flawed with current streaks or the wake of the upriver freight boats, matches their flatness. There was little of danger or difficulty for the fish in all the long river miles from Celilo to the entrance of the Snake.

The Snake comes in calmly and grandly, as a river more than a thousand miles long should come in, at the northern end of the Columbia's great curve. Chinook and Sachem had separated many miles back, Chinook towards the east bank of the river with a good part of the school behind him and Sachem holding on in the main current of the Columbia with some half-dozen other large fish. The entrance of the Snake drew Chinook almost sharply eastward, up the long smooth reach that passes under the highway bridge. Still a hundred miles west of the Washington border, he was in water that came from the farthest corners of Idaho, from Yellowstone and the beginnings of Wyoming.

Chinook mounted his river steadily, forcing the water behind him in the slow persistent swimming that the upstream salmon use. He showed seldom as he went up, holding to midwater in the deep strong channels, resting near bottom where eddies formed behind upthrusts of rock and other unevenness of the river bed. He rested once behind a pier of the great gaunt railroad bridge that crosses the river just below the entrance of the

Palouse. There were lampreys resting there in thousands, their sucking mouths used only to help them in their upstream journey, for they also were fasting before spawning. Two sturgeon, one of them a female twenty times his weight, fed near Chinook, probing the sand and shuffling across it with the gentle laziness of bottom feeders. These were familiar things of his journey and affected him not at all. He moved up from among them and passed under the skyline of the little otter-board ferry whose angled crossings use the eight-knot flow. The brown river was grand between the hard dry hills; even its forty-foot flood depth could not hide the fierce pressing of the current, and every rock and boulder on the bottom heaved the solid water to mark its line or make its foam fleck at the surface. The force that carried the sand grains along his sides was stimulation to Chinook and drew him on.

Above the ferry the wheat fields of eastern Washington occasionally reached to the river, but they seemed secure only as they moved away from it, marching their rounded hills clear to the foot of the Blue Mountains, then along and into Idaho. The winds of early June played with their infinitely shaded green and a strong sun yellowed the fall-planted fields of the year before; the polished fallows folded in browns like the nap of velvet brushed different ways. But the wheat grew from its own six full feet of topsoil and the rain that it held, owing nothing to the river. And the river turned away from such softness to draw Chinook against the race of water that pours down from Clarkston in a two-thousand-foot canyon among the bare mountains.

Chinook faced the strength of the enclosed water with his own patient strength, climbing through white water into folding glides where sheer speed of fall drew the surface to tension that had the smoothness of stretched satin, and where all the vigor of his great muscles advanced him only a foot at a time. He used the eddies behind great rocks, shouldering out into broken water again, winning new shelter only to turn out and climb on. He leapt low falls, arching forward into the taut water above them, inching up to easier water when he struck right and his tail gripped, tumbled back to try again when his leap was misjudged. And so he came out to Clarkston and the Idaho boundary.

Above Clarkston the Clearwater, muddy and fouled by dredging in its south fork, comes down by Lewiston Dam to join the Snake. No salmon turned away at the junction, only the lampreys snaked up to suck and slither their way over the new ladders at the dam—ladders that may one day carry a new race of salmon to spawn in the streams that the dam shut away from an earlier race. Chinook held to the Snake through its sharp southward curve. He rested in the shade of grain elevators, where a little town thrusts out among poplars and locusts on a tongue of flat land that forces the river hard against rocky hills. Two days later he was in the first fierce water of the Grand Canyon of the Snake, but after a little he turned from it into the Salmon River.

A great run of spring chinooks passes far up the Snake, clear through the Grand Canyon and into a hundred spawning streams beyond it. Another great run climbs far up the Salmon, spreading along its bed and searching out its far forks and tributaries. But Chinook found what he sought only three or four days after leaving the Snake; he came at evening to a great rest pool in a wide bend of the river. Tall hills climbed steeply from the water and the sun was already gone behind these and behind the mountains of the Grand Canyon. There were salmon in the pool already, not migrating fish pausing in their journey, but fish that knew the pool and had their favorite positions behind rocks and in deep places; fish that schooled sometimes, to hold quietly in midwater, circle back over the tail of the pool and move gently up again while the school gradually faded back into the holts of the individual fish. They were restless fish, rolling their backs out of the water at daylight and after sundown, jumping sometimes and circling often near the mouth of the small stream that entered at the head of the pool. Chinook stayed with these fish, even though some of those that had entered the pool with him traveled on.

The valley that fostered the stream at the head of the pool was steep and sharp, climbing three thousand feet in sloping grassland from the narrow floor of poplars that marked the stream bed. It had rock outthrusts, deep gullies, sharp folds that could hide whole companies of men and had held them, concealed and dangerous, when

Indian fought Indian and Indian fought white not so very long ago. At the head of the valley the stream climbed back into pine and hemlock and its flow was .fed by shaded creeks between the mountain ridges. Even at its mouth the stream was only a tiny babbling thing, not fifty feet across, but there were deep pools among the poplars in the valley where the maturing salmon waited for full ripeness and the first rains of fall.

A rough dirt road led down to the stream's junction with the Salmon and crossed on a plank bridge low to the water. For two days Chinook lay below the bridge, still in the bed of the big river but full in the flow of his spawning stream. Once or twice he crept up against the flow, under the safe darkness of the bridge and cautiously out again on the other side. The shallowness of the water made him nervous, constantly ready to turn in flight for the depths of the big rest pool. As he moved forward the six-foot depth under the bridge became only four feet, then shelved again and became a ripple not deep enough to cover his wide back. Once a fish darted suddenly past him, splashed over the ripple and entered the narrow deep pool beyond. Chinook moved as though to follow, swung back and forth two or three times across the lower end of the ripple, then turned and went back down under the bridge and into the main river again.

An Indian boy came to the mouth of the stream next day; he was a small boy, dark-eyed, round-faced, silent and careful on his feet. He walked across a bar of sand

and gravel to the edge of the ripple, stood there a moment, then squatted down on his haunches. He had a short spear in his hand, steel-pointed and heavily barbed, attached to a long coil of line. He watched below him, looking into the transparent brown water above the wooden bridge; there was no excitement, no impatience, no eagerness of anticipation in his face; he simply watched.

Chinook came up from the pool, under the bridge, his tail moving slowly from side to side, his eyes patient as the boy's, as little concerned with present or immediate future. Very slowly his head moved out from under the bridge, then his great shoulder and wide back, still in shadow. He turned off a little, out of the main current, and the boy saw him. The spearpoint lifted slowly from the sand, the whole spear came slowly level. Still the boy's expression had not changed; his watching was focused now and moved with Chinook's gradual ascent, but it was still utterly calm and patient. His arm drew back with the spear in smoothness that made the movement almost imperceptible. And Chinook crept on, his huge tail stirring slowly, marking the surface as he came to shallower water.

He reached the end of the eddy ten feet below the waiting boy and turned into the current. It was deeper again in the run below the ripple and he swung clear across to the far side, out of the boy's sight. The boy did not move and in a little while Chinook came back, his dorsal fin showing above the surface, his head well up in the broken water, searching the deepest way over the ripple. He came within six feet of the sandbar where the boy waited, found what he sought and started through the ripple. In one movement the boy straightened and threw his spear. It struck Chinook well forward and in the side, so that it passed below his backbone and near his heart. Chinook turned with a drive of his tail that splashed solid water from the ripple clear up into the boy's face. The boy's expression was tight and scared. Chinook ran down in the current, leaving a line of thick blood behind him in the brown water. The boy let the line drag hard, under his left foot, over a strip of rawhide on his left hand, while his right hand freed the coils.

Beyond the bridge Chinook came once to the surface and broke it white in agonized fury. Then he sounded for the deep part of the pool, felt the strength flowing from him, turned up and leapt clear out above the shine of the early morning sun on the heavy current. He fell back flat on his side with a crash that the close hills caught up. The boy saw the haft of the spear roll once slowly over above the water, and go down. He began to recover his line.

He had not smiled or changed the tenseness of his close watching. He felt that Chinook was dead, but even in death the big fish was heavy and the brown hands shook as they brought in the wet line. He saw the shine of the big body as he drew it under the bridge and brought it slowly into the eddy to his feet. Chinook lay belly up in the smooth water, without movement; the haft of the spear, resting on the sand, moved only a little in the tiny swell from the passing current. The boy reached forward, slipped his hand under a gill-cover and drew Chinook up on to the beach. Still solemn, still awed by what he had done, he knelt beside the great fish and put his hands on the wet body. For several minutes he knelt without moving.

He stood up at last and looked about him. It was still early and he saw no one; no one on the dirt road, no car on the highway that climbed through the hidden village and looped up the steep side of the valley. He looked at his fish again, persuading himself of the deep side that shaded from white belly to silver-gray, black-spotted back, of the great tail, black-spotted too, of the solid bulk and weight. The pectoral and ventral fins still quivered in the last life of mighty muscles, the body arched once, then head and tail flopped back on the sand and Chinook no longer moved in death. The boy knelt in the sand again in front of his fish, a short stick in his hand.

Very carefully he chose a wide long place where the sand was smooth and firm from the lapping of the little current waves, and began to draw with his stick. He drew without looking at Chinook, but he drew the shape of a fish with Chinook's length and Chinook's full body depth. He drew it carefully, in deep lines, but without hesitation. When he had finished and marked the eye it was not Chinook that the lines made, but the stylized type of his race that Indians have drawn and marked and carved in many ways and many places since the first Indian speared the first chinook.

## CHAPTER TWENTY

ONCE more, for the twentieth time or the fiftieth time, Spring came up to the rack. She worked along it with less patience now, turning away from it, turning sharply back, rolling heavily in the strong current so that her back showed and went down before the quickening movement of her tail. The water flowed through halfway up the bars, murmuring against them, sucking more and more strongly behind them, welling over the increasingly solid drift that wedged and packed above them.

The warm wind passed upstream, sighing with its freight of rain, finding always a stronger gust of itself to shatter the big drops from leaves that still held them. It swayed the tall firs almost gently, loading them with water, trembling the water from them again minutes later. Drenched with water the dark leaves of salal and rhododendron shone and quivered and dripped in penetrated shelter down under the tall trees. The clouds rolled up, white and gray and soft, climbing the valley and misting into the mountains. The black roads splashed the great drops and ran off water in their ditches. The creeks talked on the hillsides, turning brown and foamy and tumbling faster in their rocky beds. Far up the valley the windy rain found little pine trees, fell from them to soaked ridges, seeped from those into brimming swamps. It bowed the white bloom of the mountain laurels and melted the needle-covered patches of old snow. Last of all it found the piled snow exposed on sloping rock. It blew warmth and rained warmth, weighting the snow, turning it to coarse translucent grains, rotting it. Snow broke away from the hanging slopes and crashed downwards, melting in the warm air as it fell. It packed down as though huddling from the wind's kiss, but even where it huddled in shelter the dropping rain found it and washed it to its own mobility.

By slides and swamps, by creeks and ditches and streams it all came to the river at last, swelling the falls at the head of the canyon, sliding along the canyon walls, swelling into the Canyon Pool and quickening the strong glide over the fantail. It rolled past the Senator's house, still growing, and piled over the spillways of the dam. In the river's curves it washed the cut banks, drawing sand and boulders down and away from the roots of the heavy cedars. And it came in steadily mounting flow to the salmon rack, creeping up and up on the slats until it rode only a few inches below the crown of the tripods.

The larger drift began to come down on the third

day, battered chunks of wood, torn limbs worn smooth by water, rarely a spike-filled timber from some forgotten logging bridge or flume. The rack was well placed, in a flow that spread almost evenly from bank to bank. But little by little the drift began to collect more heavily and pile more solidly against the tripods nearest the bank where the scow was tied. A single tripod slipped a little, not more than inches, but enough to crack the wood that bound it to those on either side.

Spring and a thousand fish with her faced into the strong flow, drawing its freshness through their gills, feeling its weight on their sides and against their heads. Some fish jumped and struck against the tripods. Two or three jumped strongly forward at the right moment, cleared the rack and were free on the upstream side. Spring still searched back and forth in steady movement for a way through. Rarely she jumped, always along the fence and across the current, as though in haste to find a new place for her searching.

Half a mile upstream the flood worked far under the roots of a leaning cedar tree. The friction and suction of its passing and the little lapping waves that spread shoreward from the thrust of rocks took up the work where the winter's freshets had left it and soon found soft mud instead of gravel. The wind helped, lifting the pressure of the roots so that fingers of water crept under them, using the leverage of the tree's height and the riverward weight of its branches

The top sagged suddenly forward through several feet and stopped as suddenly, shivering a shower of water into the river. But the roots on the bank strained and groaned. One cracked and broke, then another, the water did its work and the wind still helped. Very slowly, far more slowly than before, the top moved forward again, down and down to an angle of almost forty-five degrees; then earth cracked and roots broke and tore loose. The hiss of branches gathering speed against the air met the crash of the trunk on the water, the whole root lifted clear for a moment. Then the branches broke against the bottom of the river, the trunk settled back, rolled a little, began to swing downstream and at last drew the root after it, grating against the boulders.

The tree floated the half-mile to the rack haltingly. Again and again the roots caught among the boulders and anchored it until the rising flood lifted them. Once a long root, reaching sideways, hung in the brush on the side of the river. Once the top struck a great rock in a rapid and swung the trunk against another rock, but the pull of the flood took it past these also. It came to the rack at last, almost in midstream, top first. It struck with a grating shock between two tripods, so that the top slid on over the upper brace. The root swung slowly downstream, still grinding along the bottom but with heavier and heavier force of water behind it. It struck the tripod that had already slipped, knocked it out and over, tumbled the next tripod and left a thirty-foot gap in the slats through which the water poured in solid force.

Salmon began to find the gap almost at once, passing at first in ones and twos, then in dozens, then in hundreds. Within an hour they were all free, heading upstream in the face of the freshet. Spring knew a stronger delight than she had ever known, boring up against the strong water, climbing the white rapids, seeking the heavy glides in the smooth places with all the frenzy of eagerness pent inside her by the delay and built to fullness by the flood water.

She rested that night in the shallows of the pool below the dam. The rain had stopped and the sun rose in a clear sky the next day, but the water that passed over the shallows was still strong-flowing and fresh. She moved up towards the foot of the dam, searching the racing flow below the spillways for passage. Around her in the foaming water many fish searched, boring up, gliding back, leaping in the broken waves, rolling their backs out, possessed by the need to travel while the river was strong. Spring leapt high at the heavy fall from the left spillway down which she had tumbled as a fingerling, struck less than half-way up and was hurled back. She rested in the eddy behind a buttress, turned out and leapt again at the next spillway. Through half the morning she struggled and rested alternately, leaping a dozen times in growing effort until she tired. She drifted back at last, still heading upstream, close under the right bank, and came into the flow from the ladder. She felt the flow strong about her, but went down under it and rested near bottom.

From time to time fish passed over her, heading towards the ladder. She moved at last, across the bottom, out into the rush from the spillways again. On the bank men and women stood in the sunshine and the clear, washed air, watching the salmon. Word that the rack was out had spread quickly through the valley and people came who had never before bothered to watch the salmon at the dam. They talked happily and laughed. Something in the spectacular freedom of the fish from the restraint of the great machinery of government touched them and pleased them. Little groups of men stood talking lazily of just how and where the rack should have been placed to prevent all chance of washing out. Farmers, loggers, woodsmen, fishing guides, even countermen from the stores and the telephone linemen and the drivers of delivery trucks, felt that they knew better than the government fellows because they believed they worked on more practical terms against harder reality. It was good to be able to criticize, good to see the salmon free. Senator Evans passed among the groups, talking with them, listening to them, feeling something of what they felt, more tolerant of the government fellows because he knew something of government and something of the river. They liked him and kidded him, telling him he ought to run again. A big logger, standing beside his truck, shouted: "Get back in there, Senator, so they'll have someone that knows the country right." The people laughed; many of them had been in grade school with the old man and there were farmers there who had come from New England as young men when another Old Man Evans still worked the largest of the valley's first three farms.

The groups shifted and changed. People went away and others came. The Senator stood watching the fish that passed up the ladder and the few that still jumped at the spillways. Spring worked slowly up from her resting place until she was close under the right spillway. The old man missed her first jump, but the heavy splash of her fall drew his eyes sharply from the ladder. He watched closely, waiting, and saw her clearly as she jumped again. In the quick moment he thought he saw something different about her tail, but even in her third jump he could not identify it. She did not jump again but let herself drift back in the welter of white near the surface, tumbled a little by freaks of current so that her tail came out and the old man saw clearly that there was a tag in it. He watched closely, fearing that he might have seen too easily what he was half expecting to see after the quick impression of that second jump, but she dropped back behind the ladder without showing again.

This time she did not rest. The draw of the current was strong and clear and fish after fish was passing into the ladder. She followed, climbing easily from step to step in the rush of water through the gaps. Half a dozen times her tail showed above water, slowly and steadily, and the old man watched the tag until he could almost read the number on it. He saw her pass over the last step and turned back to his car: he had come forty miles down the river from his house when they had told him the rack was out.

Spring moved in the flood current through the wide reach above the dam and rested in the first pool above the storage area. By the next day the peak of the freshet was over, but she traveled up nearly twenty miles against the rushing flow, finding easy passage through the deepened water over the steep rapids. Three days after passing the dam she came to Deer Lick Pool, half a mile below the Senator's house, in a river that was scarcely more than a foot above its normal spring height. Deer Lick Pool is in the tall virgin timber of a state forest, a strong deep glide under a cut bank, with an eddy sloping up to wide shallows, and shallows again at the tail. Spring found a place among several other chinooks, deep down near bottom in the green water. It was her summer rest pool.

## Chapter Twenty-one

WHEN Chinook turned away at the Snake, Sachem was entering the last long stage of his journey up the Columbia; it was a stage through scablands and gravel and lava and drought, through raw leavings of glacial ages that still belonged to their far distant past.

Not far above the mouth of the Snake the Yakima joins the Columbia, seeming a little river in this country of meeting giants. But the Yakima waters its land through a thousand irrigation ditches and for a few miles the dry country becomes rich green fields and spaced orchards of cherries and apples; the Columbia climbs past in sweeping breadth, back into dryness under a bright sun in a naked blue sky.

Sachem and the small school with him kept well down in the ample clouded depths of the river, safely encased in the mighty volume of cool water that crossed the barren dryness without spreading life for even a few feet beyond its banks. The sun shone hotly down on the smooth surface and was turned back upon itself before it could drive its heat more than a few inches down. All the vast breadth of heat and dryness was sharply separate from the narrow concentration of coolness and moisture that crossed it.

Above the irrigated land the fish swam for nearly a day under the sheer white faces of high clay bluffs and came beyond them into a rolling flatness of sand and gravel and sagebrush stretching away to the far ridge of Saddle Mountain. For six miles the river climbed through the ninety-foot drop of Priest Rapids and Sachem fought for many hours in powerful swimming against the pressure of flood water that smoothed the fall of the rapids into long, leaping swiftness. From the head of the rapids the wide deep cut through the long ridge of Saddle Mountain showed clearly and the river swung towards it across the sweeping desolation. Man's tiny works deserted by man spoke the barrenness and added to the desolation; the concrete foundations of little houses, the eyeless death of stone houses still standing, the emptiness of little towns made emptier by the furtive few who still moved about them, these were playthings of the shifting sand that piled below the metallic brown rock faces, eroded and worn, but not smooth. Even the sagebrush died and was buried and the rabbits kept away. The river summoned the fish through it all and sometimes thrust the green of reeds up from sandbars in shallow eddies or fostered little trees on rocky islands.

Then raw red hills came down and marched on both banks until they became rounder and smoother and at last grew grass, parched grass sandy green among lava outcrop, but rich and full of life by contrast. Sachem tasted a new freshness in the water and in a little while he came between the smooth high hills to the heavy roar of Rock Island's opened spillways.

Rock Island is the most beautiful of all the Columbia's big dams. The island itself is flat and low and lies out in midstream above the center of the dam. Between the island and the hills of the left bank there is a long line of spillway gates and near shore the big powerhouse turns upstream at an angle from them. The main dam curves strongly and gracefully from the point of the island to the right bank, buttressed on the downstream side and with a great brown rock in the center of its curve.

There are three salmon ladders at Rock Island which passed twenty or thirty thousand salmon and steelhead each year before Grand Coulee Dam was built. A ladder under the left bank draws fish that swim up in the tailrace from the powerhouse; the midstream ladder on the tip of Rock Island carries its greatest burden in low water when the fish seek the freshness of the strongest flow; and the right ladder is the way of fish that have fought vainly at high water to climb the fall over the main dam.

Sachem came to the dam in early June when the river was near its peak flow and a great glassy curve of translucent snow-green water poured without ceasing over the main dam, broken white by each buttress and shattered again to leaping white of ten-foot backward-breaking waves at the foot of its fall. He was still a perfect fish, wide and deep, unscarred by his journey, full of strength. He passed well out from the entrance of the right ladder, testing the power of the broken water below the fall. He swung across it, out towards midstream, and swung back from its growing weight. For perhaps half an hour he hung in the easy part of the race, as though measuring what he had to climb. Then he started up, shouldering through the heaving water deep under the shattered surface. He came against the foot of the fall, steadied himself in its churning distortions of current, then started for the surface with all the power and drive of his huge body. He came out in a leap that was immeasurably the noblest of his life, high above the fierce breaking of the white water and arching forward into the solid rolling wall that slid over the crown of the dam. The splash of his striking the water was swept instantly down and away, and his body showed suddenly and clearly, dark through the pale greenness. For a long half-minute he was there, holding against the river's fullest solid strength by sheer power of swimming; then he began to slip back. The tip of his tail, a tiny dark triangle, broke through the tautness of the curving water. With a tremendous effort he moved inches forward, buried it again, but he was spent. For a brief second his whole wide tail was above the surface; his body turned a little, then the current caught the side of it and swept him into the battering white below.

Bruised and tumbled, half drowned, Sachem drifted back down past the entrance of the ladder before he righted himself fully. He swung towards the shore and found resting place among broken, dynamite-scattered rocks below the ladder. He was a superbly powerful fish, moving on the peak of the flood when the height of water below the dam made the leap for the crest shorter than at any other time in the year. But he made no second try.

He moved up into the ladder at dawn of the next day and climbed the straight steps easily until a steel grating like that at Bonneville barred his way. He searched along it and almost at once found the funnel-shaped entrance to the trap. He swam through, though it was little wider than his body, and followed the current only twenty or thirty feet until he came to a second grating. Again he searched, back and forth across the whole width of the flow, but this time there was no opening wider than the two-inch space between the bars.

There were other fish in the trap; six or eight steel-head trout, perhaps ten of the precocious two-year-old male chinooks and about thirty adult chinooks—all smallish fish of fifteen or twenty pounds except the half-dozen that had traveled up with Sachem and entered the ladder the previous night. They were quiet, most of them well down in the water, facing into the flow of the current through the grating; but there were always two or three near the surface, patiently probing at the bars or circling the narrow space in the hope of finding a way to follow their journey above it; and occasionally a fish would begin to jump, coming high out of the water against the bars, driven by some sudden pressure of the urgency that had ruled it all through the long migration.

For fully an hour after entering the trap Sachem searched restlessly for a way to follow his journey, but at last he lowered himself gently through the water and lay among the other fish. A hundred and twenty miles upstream, water poured over the five-hundred-foot face of Grand Coulee Dam to crash against the great curved concrete trench below it at sixty miles an hour in torrential upheaval that no fish could face, no fry could survive. Below the fall a long tailrace ran in concentration of speed and volume with which no ladder could compete to draw the upstream fish. Sachem was a fish from somewhere in the thousand miles of spawning water above Grand Coulee, but he bore no distinguishing mark of race, no variation of shape or spots or color that could be used to separate him from fish returning to a spawning stream between the two dams—Methow or Wenatchee, Entiat or Okanogan. Since there is nowhere nearer Grand Coulee than Rock Island that fish can be trapped and held away from the destruction of the great dam, he was held there in the right ladder.

Two men came to the ladder in the afternoon. One walked out on the control platform above the trap and pressed a button, and the heavy grating that made the floor of the trap began to rise slowly through the water. Sachem felt the pressure of it, rose a little above it, felt it touch him again and moved sharply up. A steelhead ran suddenly to the surface and jumped wildly. The two men stood looking down into the trap.

One said: "Quite a few of them there. They're starting again."

The other pointed suddenly down. A big fish had come near the surface and was searching in the current close to the bars. "Look at that, Dave. The hogs must be starting."

Dave nodded, still looking down. Other big fish were beginning to show as the brail moved up. Then Sachem showed, swimming slowly and sulkily above the brail. "Holy cow," Dave said. "Would you look at that baby. He'll need a truck all to himself." He looked up at his companion. "O.K.?" he asked.

"Sure. There's a load there. Looks as though there'll be two by tomorrow morning, but we'll take them then anyway."

Dave leaned back and pressed a button and the grill began to go down again. "Guess they'll be coming strong to this side for a day or two, Johnny. There wasn't much in the left trap this morning."

"I'm surely glad they're here," Johnny said. "Don's coming over tomorrow with old Senator Evans and I promised to show him something."

"Don Gunner? Where does that guy get his pull, running all over the country with senators? I thought he had a job down in Oregon."

Johnny laughed. "Don't worry about Don. He'll earn his trip. I've been trying since God knows when to get him up here to show me some of those ideas he's using in Oregon."

As the brail went down under him Sachem went down, seeking the security of the snow-stained water. The confinement of the trap, the gentle pressure of the brail, the movement of figures above him had all made him afraid. He was not panicky, but cautious and nervous, and when the brail stopped again at the bottom of the trap he settled close to it, holding in utter stillness to let the danger pass away from him.

## Chapter Twenty-two

Two small Bureau of Fisheries trucks, one Gunner's, one Johnny's, came down to the trap early next morning. It was sunny there, with a strong wind blowing across the river, and the dam was beautiful, long and low and gleaming in the clear light. The four men walked over to the trap and stood against the high structure of the elevator to be out of the wind. Dave started the brail up from the bottom of the trap and Gunner and Johnny and the Senator watched. The fish began to show and Dave stopped the brail. Johnny said: "The truck won't be along for a while yet, so we may as well leave them there for now."

Dave came and looked into the trap. The water was

still deep over the brail but they could see a dozen or more fish crowding against the grating that stopped the way through the ladder on the upstream side. "Looks like another bunch came in after we were here yesterday," Dave said. "There's almost a load in the left trap too."

The Senator looked down at the fish. The wide backs of the thirty-pounders and the gentle persistence with which they pressed their noses to the gaps in the grating fascinated him. A big red-sided steelhead jumped, splashing water up, and Dave lowered the grating a little. Then they saw the tank truck coming down the hill, its aluminum paint bright in the sun, and Dave switched the current flow so that it came into the trap through the shaft of the elevator instead of down the ladder.

Sachem had felt the pressure of the brail and had risen with it, but he kept down as far as he could, not wanting to show himself as he had before. He was suspicious and sulky, ready to resist or flee from anything that threatened him. In some measure he was used to the trap; he knew he could not get away from it downstream and he had little desire to do so; it held him from going upstream, but so long as the flow of water drew down through it he could find a measure of relief from fear in searching a way up against it or in simply facing into it. He felt the sudden change of the flow, striking against his side instead of against his head and along his body, and turned towards it at once. His pectorals quivered and the motion of his tail quickened. Very slowly he moved up from the brail towards the bars between the trap and the elevator shaft.

The tank truck had backed under the elevator chute and Johnny was showing Senator Evans its perfections. The wind tore his words away as he spoke them and the roar of water over the dam submerged them. "Twelve hundred pounds of ice"—he lifted a round hatch between the tank and the cab. "Air sucked over it—engines down here," he pointed low on the side of the truck, behind the cab. "Two of them—in case one goes haywire. Then pumped through the bottom of the tank. Lowers temperature of water on the trip. Thousand gallons in tank—enough for about fifty chinooks on the trip to Nason Creek."

They moved back and the truck shot the stale water from the tank through a circular rear door. Dave raised the elevator and dumped a thousand gallons of fresh water through the chute into the tank, to cushion the fish when they came down from the elevator in another thousand gallons. Then he lowered the elevator again. Gunner called from the side of the trap and Johnny went down with the Senator. "Look," Gunner said.

Sachem was well up in the water, facing the strong flow through the elevator, pressing against the bars, searching across them, raising his great neb out of the water and letting it slide down against the gaps. His movements were deliberate, almost systematic, and his search was thorough. Dave came from his controls to watch and the truck driver came. Johnny said: "Have you got fish like that down in Oregon, Senator?"

The old man looked up at him and smiled. "Not many," he said. "That fish is better than sixty pounds."

"Don't let it worry you," Johnny said. "We don't see them like that often either, do we, Dave?"

The Senator watched Sachem still trying to find a way through the bars. Other fish near him were trying with the same persistence. "You can darn near hear that fellow think," the old man said. "He's just going to find a way through those bars or wear his nose out trying."

Dave raised the brail until the sloping part of it came near the top of the water on the river side of the trap. Then he opened the funnel-shaped entrance from the trap to the elevator. Two little jacks passed through at once, with a fifteen-pound chinook close behind them. Sachem still probed at the bars, working along them towards the opening. He found the entrance, started over the reflecting plate, turned sharply back, then came again and passed through, slowly and cautiously. For nearly half a minute his great tail swayed back and forth, still over the counting plate, then swirled once and disappeared into the elevator. The men watching felt a tension relax from them and Dave laughed. "It's always like that," he said. "No matter how many times you see it it's still exciting." Fish went through steadily for a little while, then the movement slowed. Dave raised the brail until the sloping side was well above water, crowding the fish towards the entrance, and several more moved in. Still looking down at the counting plate he said: "Forty chinooks, with the big baby. Four steelhead. Three suckers. Seven jacks."

"Let it go at that," Johnny said. "Several of those chinooks are big and it looks as though there won't be more than a load for tomorrow morning."

In the elevator Sachem turned again into the flowing water and came again against a steel grating. He felt the elevator rising, and the flooding of water out through the bars let him down into the solid thousand-gallon box at the base. Then suddenly water was rushing past him in a new direction. He turned into it with unbelievable quickness and fought it with all his strength. It drew away from him, leaving his tail exposed and he slid out on to the chute and slowly down, tail first, into the truck. The sliding cover drew over the top of the tank, men's hands splashing the water in the narrowing gap to keep the fish down. In the bubbling darkness Sachem was quiet. The throb of the little auxiliary engine was drowned by the truck starting. All the fish were quiet, huddled together in the bottom of the tank; the water slopped against the cover and dripped back; the cool bubbles came up through the bottom of the tank in steady streams that dissolved oxygen into the water.

The truck passed through Wenatchee's busy streets,

out along the highway, then swung up the Wenatchee Valley at its steady twenty miles an hour, climbing through the orchards towards tall hills with snow and timber on them. Still down at the dam, Johnny worked at the back of his truck, testing a water sample he had taken from the trap. Senator Evans stood in the windy sun, his tall old body straight and firm, watching the roll of water over the crest of the dam. He asked Dave: "Do you suppose a fish could make it against that?"

"We wonder a bit sometimes," Dave said. "Of course, it's about peak flow now—two hundred and seventy thousand cubic feet a second today, and they say it won't go over that this year. One year the spring run-off was seven hundred and fifty thousand, and if that happened I guess there would be hardly any drop at the dam. Johnny thinks they'd make it all right then."

"That might mean a year's run would be lost up under Grand Coulee."

"Yes—unless they were established in the streams below Grand Coulee by then. We're hoping that after six or seven years of catching the run down here and planting natural spawners and hatchery fry in the streams between here and Coulee we'll get a run that won't want to go on up. If that happened we could lay off the trucks and let the fish go through the ladders again."

Johnny finished his tests and Gunner and the Senator piled into the little Fisheries truck with him to follow the tank truck. For a while the two biologists talked their shop, then Johnny said: "What did you think of it, Senator?"

"I'm just plain impressed by all the thoroughness," the old man said. "What were those tests you made with the water sample?"

"We take temperature, alkalinity, carbon dioxide and oxygen," Johnny said. "I'll do it again when he stops half-way, then again when we get to Nason Creek."

"Do you do that every trip?"

"No, not more than once or twice a week as a check and to give us some figures to work on for any future work that's a bit different. The drivers carry thermometers of course and check once in a while on every trip to be sure that things are working right."

Don said: "What about the hatchery, Johnny? Finished yet?"

"Leavenworth, you mean? No, but they won't be long; they say they mean to take most of the hog-run off us. You ought to see Leavenworth, Senator. Handles a hundred million eggs. A dozen rearing ponds that will look like full-sized lakes when they get them finished, holding pools for spawners like this lot to ripen in, stripping sheds, seining racks, even elevators so we can truck spawned-out steelhead back to the main river. Big-time stuff that belongs right with Grand Coulee. They've even got a pipe line from some cold lakes way up in the hills in case Icicle Creek warms up too much in the summer."

Don said: "We can take a look at it on the way back from Nason Creek, can't we, Johnny? The Senator wants to see some of those revolving fish screens too."

"Those are the clear rig," Johnny said. "They've got them all through Yakima Valley and we're pretty well fixed with them up this way. When you figure the numbers of young fish those are going to keep from going along the irrigation ditches to fertilize farmers' orchards, and then all the old spawning water that's being reopened by putting proper ladders at little haywire dams, you've got something that's going to make a difference. I think there's a real chance the Columbia runs may build up from now on if they keep the fishing controlled, don't you, Don?"

Don nodded. "I don't see why not," he said. "Those are positive gains and it seems as though the big dams aren't going to do much harm, thanks to you fellows."

"We've been lucky," Johnny said. "The fish have done just about what we hoped they'd do. But we aren't out of the woods yet. The fry and fingerlings have got to get down and back again before we'll know anything for certain."

They came up with the truck at its half-way stop and Johnny made his second set of tests. Sixty miles from Rock Island, well up in the mountains towards Stevens Pass, the truck stopped again at a gravel turnout beside Nason Creek. The Senator stepped out and felt the cold wind from the snows in spite of the June sun. From the dry hills near the dam he was back among timber again; the head of the Wenatchee Valley was not so very different from his own coast valley where Spring lay in her summer rest pool. The old man walked out on the ramp that led the trucks over the water and looked down into a deep pool with big boulders on the bottom. Johnny stood beside him. "There's six miles of first-class spawning water here in Nason Creek," he said. "We've got it fenced some way upstream of here and down near where it joins the Wenatchee."

"How many fish do you put in?"

"Last year we had a thousand steelhead and more than three thousand spring-run chinooks. We put most of the hog-run down in a length of the Wenatchee that's fenced off the same way, and I guess we'll do it again this year if Leavenworth doesn't take them. The bluebacks go up to Osoyoos Lake above the Canadian border—that's a hundred-and-sixty-mile run, and the trucks have to take fresh ice before the end of the trip."

The driver started his engine again and the two men moved off the ramp. The truck backed slowly out to the end of the ramp so that the metal chute clamped under the rear door of the tank was well out over the water. Johnny climbed up to take his water sample and the Senator went up with him to look at the fish.

Sachem's great nose came up, exploring the narrow opening, and Johnny pushed him down. "You have to watch them," he said. "They'll jump if they can. Dave got a forty-pounder full in the face one day—slapped him right off the truck." He closed the sliding door and they climbed down again.

Inside the tank Sachem went back down to the bottom of the darkness and lay facing forward towards the cab. The driver tripped the rear door of the tank and instantly he was fighting a rush of water again. A few fish, caught off balance, were carried out almost at once; most of them held until the water drew away and they could no longer swim properly, then slid, flopping and struggling, down the chute. Sachem was last of all. Even before he struck the surface of the pool he was swimming and in the water he straightened himself instantly to face the good cool flow. He held about two feet under water behind a big rock near the head of the pool and they watched him. The Senator said: "That's the finest fish I've ever seen, bar none."

Johnny said: "They don't come much better. I wonder which way he'll go, up or down."

The truck driver said: "It's funny. I get just as much kick out of seeing those babies as I did the first trip. That big one sure is a honey, but I guess he wouldn't look so big if he was with the rest of the hogs."

Don said: "He'd look big any place except in a

school of whales. If that fish doesn't go close to eighty pounds I miss my guess."

Johnny turned away, Don and the Senator followed him to the small truck. The driver of the tank truck waved to them as they started, then took his lunch out of the cab and went down to eat it on the ramp, where he could watch Sachem. At last he too went away.

Sachem lay quietly behind the big rock through most of the afternoon. He had settled deeper in the water and occasionally he turned out into the flow of current on one side or other of the rock; once or twice he came up to the surface and rolled. Towards evening he grew more restless. Fish were passing him on their way up out of the pool. For some reason, perhaps because Nason Creek was not sufficiently like his own stream, the desire to climb against the current had left him and he turned down. He came to another pool, swam through it and followed down to a pool where twenty or thirty fish were collected. Here he rested through the night, but early the next morning he started again, and about a dozen fish went with him. They swam down, resting in the pools sometimes, but never for very long, and before evening they came to the rack at the lower end of the spawning reach. Sachem searched along the wooden slats for a way through, found the wide entrance of a trap and went down into it. The lower end of the trap was closed and for a while he lay there quietly under the shade of the slats that covered it, facing upstream. Then he worked slowly up again and came out to lie above the fence among several hundred other fish.

Through June and July and most of August Sachem lay there above the lower fence in Nason Creek, and Johnny watched him often on his rounds. Other fish came down until there were nearly a thousand collected there in solid swaying lines over the shallows. Sometimes they spread upstream a little, but they were never very far from the fence. Below the other fence, at the head of the spawning water, almost as many fish had collected, and perhaps a thousand others were scattered through the reach. Sachem's great milt sacs developed steadily and the savage hook grew in his lower jaw. His color changed; his back grew darker, almost black, and the whiteness of his belly became dirty over the bulging milt. His body was no longer so wide with thick muscle. Towards the end of August he grew more and more restless. Fish began to move upstream from the fence, scattering over the spawning beds. Sachem went up, finding his irritable way from pool to pool, from nesting female to nesting female. He stopped at last behind a good-sized female who had an egg-pocket almost completed. Three smaller males lay near her. Sachem chased the largest away and slid into position beside the female, his great head near her shoulder. One of the small males came too close, Sachem turned to chase him, followed only a little way, and came back to the female. He touched her gently with his nose and slid alongside her again, this time well up so that her head was only a little past his dorsal fin.

## CHAPTER TWENTY-THREE

WHILE Sachem lay above the rack in Nason Creek, Spring lay in Deer Lick Pool two hundred and fifty miles to the south. The sun was hot above the tall timber and the river dropped away down to its summer level, but the running green depths under the cut bank were always cool and she moved from them only to seek the shallows of the pool at night. Hour after hour through day after day she lay quietly near bottom, her body swaying gently in the stream, all desire gone from her in the concentration of the slow development of the eggs within her. Very occasionally she came to the surface and rolled, once or twice she jumped right out as though stirred by sudden impatience. But while the crash of her fall still echoed among the tall trees, she was back near the bottom of the pool, at rest in her chosen place.

Senator Evans came to the pool several times during the summer, searching it with his floating flies to draw the big rainbows up from their feeding in the deep fast water. Once, when he had waded across the sloping shallows to the edge of the deep water, he rose and hooked a good fish up at the head of the run. The fish jumped strongly, ran up a little way, then came back fast into the body of the pool. The old man picked up line and drew the fish across close behind Spring's tail. The flash in the water so near her stirred something in Spring and she turned and followed the trout almost to the Senator's feet. He saw her clearly, then the trout turned sharply and she fled back into deep water, frightened. The old man netted his fish, still looking towards where he had seen her. Then he shook his head. "Must be something wrong with my eyes," he said. "Every time I see a chinook I see a tag in its tail."

But he left his rod and net at the edge of the water, waded across the tail of the pool and climbed the high bank on the other side to look down to the bottom of the deep run. The light was bad; he could make out the moving shapes of fish from time to time, but he could not see them clearly. And though he came back again on other days when he could see the fish well, he did not satisfy himself that any one of them carried a tag.

The summer life waxed in the pool around Spring, passing through all the phases that had ruled her early life in the Canyon Pool—the mayflies and stoneflies and sedges hatched, green algae grew thickly, diatoms multiplied, rotifers and flagellates followed through their quickening life cycles. These things, even the movement of trout and young chinooks in the pool about her and the splashings of a female merganser hunting with her brood, did not touch Spring. She lay as though conserving her strength, waiting for full ripeness. Her body changed little in appearance, though her ovaries grew and swelled, spreading their pressure along her belly to the vent, distending her flanks, gradually changing her balance by drawing the stored fat and protein from her flesh. Her back remained gray-green, her belly white, her head small, her whole body shape strong and graceful in spite of the shift of weight to her body cavity.

By the middle of August she was growing more restless, rolling more often, sometimes circling almost sharply downstream and back to her position. One evening towards the end of the month she moved to the head of the pool and held there a long while, well up in the fast water just below the fall of the rapid. That night a heavy rainstorm swept along the tall mountains, setting the creeks to murmuring over their dry beds; it was not enough to raise the river perceptibly, but it freshened the flow that came down to Spring. She felt the slight change, in her mouth and gills and along the tubed, sensitive lines at the sides of her body. As the light came down through timber and mist to the face of the pool she began to move. At first she only raised herself from the bottom into the full flow of the fast current and held there, poised on vibrant fins. Then the motion of her tail quickened and she slipped forward, up the pool. She passed up into the rapid in a little rush that sent a ripple ahead of her against the waves and swam on steadily through the deepest channels she could find.

Half an hour later she passed through the pool in the bend by the Senator's house, came out of it into the rapid above and still climbed. All the strongest urgency of her upstream journey in May was back with her and the broken force of the rapid matched and redoubled the mounting of forces inside her. She reached another pool, followed its strongest run to the head and began to work up over the wide shallow bar at the tail of the rapid below the Canyon Pool. Her dorsal fin and part of her back came above the surface and her belly slid over the rounded stones of the bar, shifting the pressure of her ovaries in pleasant sensation that urged her to struggle more strongly even than before. She crossed the shallowest place lying half over on her side and came to deeper water again. A few minutes later she followed her own broad ripple into the smooth slow glide of the Canyon Pool. She swam up the shallow fantail without pausing and slid into deep water not twenty feet out from the brown rock in the eddy above which she had fed in her first year. Behind her, other fish came into the pool.

Spring was restless in the Canyon Pool. She schooled with the other fish that came there, circling and holding in midwater over the deepest part of the pool. She went back over the shallows at the tail, stirring the brown diatom growth from the rocks, swaying back and forth in the flow, now drifting down with her body slightly across the stream, now swimming back to deep water. Within a few days there were fifty or more chinooks in the pool, all restlessly searching, sometimes rolling, sometimes jumping, seldom still. One other fish besides Spring bore a tag—the one that had been caught with her from the *Kathleen*, off the coast of Vancouver Island. He was seldom near her and she made no move at any time to be near him. Whatever it was that had held the two fish together through so many years of their lives had been completely broken by their separation in the tailrace of the mill.

The Senator came to the pool early in September and watched the fish from his seat against the rock wall. For one more year they would spawn as they were meant to spawn, and fry and fingerlings would grow from their spawning as they were meant to grow, from the natural abundance of the river. And the rack might go out again or they might decide against using it another year. He played with his hopes, but he felt in his heart that he was seeing the end of it, the last natural spawning of the chinooks that belonged to his river. He thought of what his father had said as they came down the river on a wet September day nearly sixty years earlier: "If you and I spent less time watching fish and more time on the farm we'd be a whole lot richer, young fellow." But they hadn't stopped watching them and here he was still watching them,

in spite of sixty years and the rack and a thousand gill-
nets down in the Columbia.

The old man stayed a long while at the pool, watching the fish carefully to see if any bore tags. Spring
was well over and deep in the water and he did not
see her. But he saw the other tagged fish clearly. He
tried to see the adipose and ventral fins, using the
glasses, but after a little while he put them down and
shook his head. It was impossible to see certainly, but
he knew it was too much to hope that the millionth
chance had come back to him. He got up at last and
went down towards his house.

Almost as he left, Spring drifted back on to the shallows at the tail of her pool. She was ripe now and the
eggs were shed from her ovaries into her body cavity.
Two or three other females were already digging nests
on the shallows and males hung close below them.
Spring crossed downstream of them towards the right
bank, then searched slowly up until she was under five
or six feet of water. She moved restlessly a little more
towards the bank, let herself drift back several feet,
then turned sharply on her side and thrust strongly with
her tail. The movement swept the brown diatoms from
the rocks in a cloud and moved a little sand which settled back quickly. She turned again, her tail fanning
rapidly in vigorous strokes that stirred sand and gravel
and drove her forward sharply.

By the next morning she was well on with her nest-
making and two males had settled in patient waiting

below her. A third joined them, moved away, came back and waited too. Small trout moved over the gravel among the males, picking up mayfly nymphs and chironomids and caddis disturbed by Spring's digging. Spring's fine body turned and flashed and arched upwards in repeated thrusts that broke away surface crust and worked down into looser gravel below. A male of ten or twelve pounds moved close to her and another twice his size chased him away and came back to where he had been. The nest was deep now and Spring let herself gently back in the current until her anal fin was over it. The male moved up to her side and his body quivered. Spring felt him near her, but the nest was not ready and she turned again, stirring more of the sand and loose stones from the bottom of it. An excitement possessed her so that from time to time she opened her mouth and gulped water through her gills. She dug again, drifted back again and the male moved close to her. His nose touched her tail and she made a quick movement as though to dart away, but held while he slipped along her side. She felt his body close against her, felt the eggs in her own body pressing her swollen vent; the male quivered. In the moment Spring raised her head, mouth wide open, and arched her body. The male's mouth opened and the two fish shuddered milt and gleaming eggs together into the nest.

The male dropped back almost at once and Spring began digging again, covering the eggs and starting a new nest a little upstream. She was held in the rigid grip of her purpose, utterly unconscious of other females on other redds near her or of the males that maneuvered and fought for position behind her. Every movement and phase of her life on her own redd, digging or resting or shedding eggs, was strongest, long-sought satisfaction, realization of steadily growing desires that had drawn her through six hundred miles of salt water and along three rivers to the Canyon Pool.

Four days after Spring began spawning there were a dozen females on redds at the tail of the pool, nearly all with adult males and jacks behind them. From time to time fish moved up into the pool from rest pools farther downstream and occasionally another female, feeling her ripeness, dropped back from the deep water and began searching over the shallows, often digging in several places as though testing the gravel before finally choosing a place for her redd.

In the late evening of that day a black bear came down to the river through the alders and second-growth fir. At the edge of the water he paused for a moment, lifted his forepaws from the rocks and squatted on his haunches, wet black muzzle raised to the wind. Then he lowered himself and went out into the water on all fours, wading just where the pool broke into the rapid. When the water was well up on his shoulders he stopped again and squatted back. His forepaws were free and ready, just below the surface, and he held his head high, looking a little downstream of him, turning only occasionally.

The bear had moved through the water smoothly and quietly. Spring, a hundred feet upstream, had seen not even a ripple from his movement and the males below her had not moved. A little inshore of her and twenty feet downstream another female had held to her nesting. A single male waited below her, the fish that had been tagged with Spring off Vancouver Island. He had moved upstream as the bear passed, impatiently rather than nervously. He was restless, swimming up towards the female every so often and dropping back. A smaller male moved near her and he chased it off. The smaller male came back, chased a jack, then circled close to the female again. The tagged fish ran at him, held close after him as he turned along the lip of the pool. The bear seemed to sense the passing of the first fish too late, but his paws flashed under water and gripped the tagged fish firmly. He lifted the heavy, twisting body out of the water, holding it securely between both paws, and bit once through the backbone, a little behind the head. Then he waded ashore, dragging the fish in his mouth. At the edge of the water he stopped and fed, taking the flesh from the thick part of the body between the head and the dorsal fin; then he dragged the rest of the fish a few yards up the bank and went back into the water.

Two days later Senator Evans came up to the pool. He saw the bear's beaten trails among the ferns and the remains of fish he had eaten and dragged. He found the carcase of the tagged fish and had lifted the tail with the toe of his shoe before he saw the tag. He bent down and tore it away easily through the already softening flesh between the rays of the tail, looked at it closely and read the number. Then he looked at the carcase again and saw that the adipose fin was still there, and both ventrals. He slipped the tag into the pocket of his coat and went on to the blackened stump from which he had watched Spring's dam spawning.

Leaning against the stump he took the tag from his pocket and looked at it again, turning it over in his fingers. The number told him nothing, but he guessed that "B. C." on the reverse side stood for British Columbia. "Close, anyway," he told himself. "Perhaps even the same year. What a pity the fins were all there." He raised his eyes to watch the fish on the redds. At first it was not easy to see them, but his eyes grew used to the light and the shifting streaks of current on the surface and he saw that there were spawning females all across the tail of the pool. As had happened six years earlier, the angle of the light was best through the strip of water where Spring had her redd, and the old man settled himself to watch her closely.

After nearly a week on the redd Spring was still a strong fish. Most of her eggs were safely buried under the freshly turned gravel behind her, but she had begun a new nest and was resting over it. As the old man watched she moved forward and began digging again, lifting the gravel with her strong tail so that it came up into the current above the pocket and was carried back, the larger stones only a little, smaller stones farther and the sand farthest of all, scattering over the rest of the redd. The old man took out his field glasses and focused them carefully, hoping that he might perhaps see again the whole spawning. But after a little while she stopped digging, dropped back over the egg-pocket and rested. The waiting male moved up very slowly, swinging gradually across until he came behind a female who had almost completed the first pocket of her redd. Two other males were behind her, scarred fish that were already beginning to grow weak, and he ran at them and chased them away; when they came back he had already worked up very close to the female, his body quivering as he sought to hasten her spawning.

But the old man could not see the fish clearly through the water and he turned his glasses back on Spring. She was still resting. He held the glasses on her head, watching the movement of her mouth, the almost imperceptible opening and closing of her gills, then turned them back along her body, trying to see more exactly how deep was the egg-pocket and what was her position over it. It was not easy to make out her lower fins against the pale gravel but he thought he could see that her anal fin was well over the pocket, held down in it. He moved the glasses a fraction of an inch farther, to watch the gentle, easy movement of her tail and then he saw the tag, clearly and distinctly. He could not have felt so sure had he not held a tag in his hands a few minutes before, but with that help he knew instantly that it was a tag he saw and not a scar or chance mark of any kind. He set the glasses down and stood up straight. It would probably be simple to snag her by casting a heavy gang hook across her back and drawing it sharply into her side. In less than an hour he could get down to the house, pick up a rod and be back at the pool ready to try. He leaned forward on the stump again and picked up the glasses. The fish was still strong and unmarked, on an uncompleted redd. He looked closely at her fine body, the width and breadth and depth of it, its calm security in good water at the climax of a life of constant danger. He looked for the adipose and left ventral fins and convinced himself that he saw them both; he looked back at the ventral and felt less certain, then at the adipose again and the shortened perspective of the glasses brought a small dark pebble, lying beyond Spring, into the exact position of the fin above her back. So he knew that the adipose was there and the ventral must be too.

He did not hesitate for a moment about his decision. This was a fine female on an uncompleted redd. She bore a tag, but he had already found one tag; she was not one of his own marked fish, and it seemed unlikely that by killing her he would add much to the knowl-

edge that was already secure. Finally she would be on
the redd for several more days and it might even be
easier to get her then, as she grew weak. He looked at
her again through the glasses, for a long time. Then he
turned away and started home.

It rained that night and for three days and nights
after. Spring completed the last pocket of her redd,
spawning for the first time with a male larger than
herself, straining with intense, satisfying effort to force
the last eggs from her. She lay at the head of the finished redd, digging sometimes, resting often with little
movement for hours on end. All power of vigorous
activity had gone from her with the completion of the
last egg-pocket and the strength that held her upright
and secure in the heavy water was flowing from her
fast. The river rose steadily, bringing the year's dead
and dying leaves with it, staining itself gray-brown as
it brushed clay banks and took in the flood of its
creeks.

Spring felt the strengthening flow and some faint
urgency still within her responded, quickening the
beat of tail and body that held her in position at the
head of her redd. But the weakness swung her at last
and the current gripped her and carried her back. She
felt the touch of the rocks at the break of the rapid,
righted herself and fought back into the pool. For a
long while she rested in deep water, above her redd
and towards the bank from it. The current pulled at
her again and she angled across it, swung into the eddy

and turned behind the brown boulder. There she waited while life drew away from her and the river swelled browner and stronger.

Senator Evans knew he had missed his chance of recovering Spring's tag when he saw the rain start. He was away from the river, down in the main valley, for nearly a week. When he came back to the pool he went straight to the rock wall and stood there, looking down at the brown water where the eddy welled up and back along the heavy straight flow from the canyon. As he watched a spent fish rolled weakly, almost at his feet. It rolled again, very slowly, right at the edge of the current, and he saw it clearly: head, back, dorsal fin, then the tag against the frayed white rays of the tail. No adipose fin; he saw that clearly and knew he had seen it, for the image of suspended movement was sharp and brilliant in his mind; the wet black back above the brown water and the length behind the dorsal fin exaggerated by its blankness. He could close his eyes and see it again, even to the little pale scar where the fin had been. But it could only be an image for him alone, closed within himself, to be summoned to vivid life whenever he wished to see it. Showing at his feet in the brown water she had been utterly beyond reach of any quickness of thought or action that would have made concrete the fact of her far journey and faithful return.

The strong current caught Spring as she went down from the surface. It drew her to itself, rolled her over and swept her on and she no longer resisted. Her tail moved once or twice, feebly, but all the urgencies, all the desires that had driven life through her were spent. So she lay quietly across the stream flow, drifting, as no strong salmon does; and the water opened her gill plates and forced under them and she died.

THE END